HOME G ROWN

Advice on growing your own vegetables

Contents

All rights reserved.

No part of this publication may be reproduced, stored in a retrieval system or transmitted by any means (electronic, mechanical, photocopying or otherwise) without the prior permission of the publisher.

Originally published in 2010 by L&K Designs. This edition published for Myriad Books Limited. Text by Margaret Bradley.
© L&K Designs 2010
PRINTED IN CHINA

Publishers Disclaimer

Whilst every effort has been made to ensure that the information contained is correct, the publisher cannot be held responsible for any errors and or omissions. Please note certain recipes may contain nuts or nut oil.

Why grow your own?

There is nothing to compare to growing, picking and eating your own home produce! Whether you have acres to cultivate, a small garden or an allotment, the taste of just picked vegetables, coupled with the considerable benefits to your health and your pocket will soon reap rewards. We all know that prevalent research and studies have determined a link between ill health and poor diet and a lack of exercise.

Growing your own vegetables therefore effectively kills these two birds with one stone! Even if you don't have space in your garden, there is nothing to stop you planting a small harvest in pots and containers. If you are new to gardening or want to introduce the benefits of growing your own to children, containers and pots are a manageable place to start. A small vegetable patch, with a little work, can produce a plentiful harvest, and if you are unable to dedicate an area in your garden solely to vegetables try planting produce between your blooms in your flowerbeds!

If once you have begun you feel that you need a bigger area, step up to perhaps an allotment, or share of an allotment. Be warned that these are often hard to come by, but in the UK the National Trust now offers allotments on its land, along with many towns and cities running community garden schemes.

Included in the book are a selection of recipes incorporating a few of the vegetables that you may grow. When it comes to choosing your crops, there is obviously no point in growing vegetables that you don't want to eat, but if the list of vegetables you like is too exhaustive, try planting the "colours of the rainbow". The various colours that nature provides in fruit and vegetables represent essential nutrients. The more colours you eat the more vitamins and minerals you ingest.

Colour/Vegetable	Benefits
Red e.g strawberries, tomatoes, beets, cranberries etc	Lowers blood pressure, reduces cholesterol levels, reduces the risk of cancers, protecting the body from free radicals.
Orange/Yellow e.g carrots, pumpkins, grapefruits etc	Reduces the affects of aging, lowering cholesterol and blood pressure, fighting free radicals and improving collagen formation and promoting healthy bones and joints.
Green e.g broccoli, Brussel sprouts, spinach etc	Reduces the risk of certain cancers, lowers cholesterol and blood pressure, boosting the immune system and helping to maintain retinal health.
White e.g cauliflower, garlic, parsnips etc	Boosting the immune system, balancing hormone levels and helping to reduce the risk of certain cancers.
Blue/Purple e.g aubergine, blueberries etc	Improves digestion, assisting mineral absorption, helps lower cholesterol, helps to fight against cancer cells and has anti-inflammatory properties.

Finally, the book includes a planting diary for you to use - you can of course create your own more comprehensive record, but this is to get you started

Planning

There are many reasons to have an allotment or vegetable patch. For some it is a traditional activity handed down through generations. For others, it is an essential part of maintaining a healthy balanced diet, particularly given the increasing cost to the environment of chemical based mass farming.

Others choose to grow their own fruit and vegetables or run an allotment for economic reasons - whichever reason is forefront in your mind when you decide to try your hand at "home-grown", the benefits will encompass all of the above and provide a wonderful sense of achievement when you harvest your own food.

In addition to the taste and health benefits of eating organic fresh vegetables and fruit, the maintenance of a vegetable patch or allotment provides regular exercise whilst working in the open air - much cheaper than the local gym!

When taking on a vegetable patch or allotment, you need to be realistic about your aims and capabilities. It also pays, in the main, to try to be realistic about any help you may get from family and friends. Take into account that the novelty of a vegetable patch or allotment may wear off for helpers, and bear this in mind when deciding your goals.

Remember that a vegetable patch or allotment is a commitment and regular care is essential, not just on sunny days. Once you have decided how much or how little you want to do and created a plan and budget to suit this, you may find that growing your own vegetables and fruit is less daunting than you first imagined.

If your garden is not big enough to grow the yield of vegetables and fruit you would like, contact your local council as most allotments in the UK are council-owned. Be prepared, however to join a waiting list given the resurgent popularity of vegetable gardening.

When choosing your allotment try and pick a site that has an easily accessible water supply and adequate site security, including a secure hut for storing your tools. If your chosen site has an association, this can bring additional benefits and opportunities from the bulk purchasing of materials to a network of supporters and volunteers.

You should also consider the location of your allotment in relation to your home - the closer to your home the better, not only will it be easier to dash off and dig some vegetables on a regular basis for dinner, but also if you have to travel a considerable distance, you need to take into account travel expenses. Once you have found your plot, you will be required to sign a tenancy agreement. The full site details and restrictions, if any, will be included in this agreement which would normally run for an initial period of 12 months. Site rent is normally payable in advance.

As a rough guide, a standard size plot is around 250sq metres (300sq yards) but many sites will allow plots to be split into smaller, more manageable plots. Generally most sites will not allow for the allotment to be run as a business or for you to sub-let the plot, so if you think that a full size plot will be too hard to manage to begin with, then make your requirements for a reduced size plot clear at the outset.

In the first instance, the start-up costs of an allotment can be relatively small, but it is easy to get carried away and purchase unnecessary items. Even if you have no tools, you can begin to tend your allotment with a spade and a few packets of seeds. Greenhouses, sheds, edging beds, fruit cages and watering systems are all things that can be added to your allotment over the years - don't feel the need to splash out on these to begin with. If you are lucky enough to take over a plot that has been well maintained or just recently abandoned you will probably need only to clear away the residue of any recent crop, whereas a long neglected plot or new vegetable garden made from where there was previously a lawned area, will require considerably more work.

Remember that you can reassess your aims and goals at any time, and if your plot is in need of a lot of work, it is sensible to start with a small area. Also bear in mind that if you leave a large cleared area for too long, weeds will resurface and negate the hardwork you have done. If your plot is turfed, this can be removed relatively easily using a sharp spade - but if your area is substantial, you might find it better to hire a turf-cutting machine. If you know of a friend who needs a new lawn why not enlist their help - you may find they would be prepared to do the work for you in return for taking the turf!

If you can start the work in the autumn, this will give you the entire winter season to clear and prepare the area. If you start this during the growing season this will be harder, and in this instance you should identify the least overgrown part of the plot and begin here. Now you've got your allotment, do absolutely nothing! Take a day out to assess the plot and try to visualise how you would like your allotment to be. If you can, spend the entire day at your allotment so that you can monitor the fall of light and shade in the different areas of your plot so that you can sow crops accordingly.

Assessing the soil

Remove any weeds and dig a small square hole, roughly 45cm (18in) in depth and width. This will show the quality of both the topsoil and the lower subsoil. Pour water into the hole to the depth of about 10cm (4in) and record how long it takes for the water to drain away. If the water drains steadily and quickly disappears then drainage shouldn't be a problem. The longer it takes for the water to drain, the more likely that you may need to undertake preliminary drainage to avoid waterlogging.

Regular cultivation and the addition of organic material can cure a drainage problem. Remember if you are working on an allotment that the other gardeners on your plot will have experience of working with the soil, so ask their advice. Likewise, if you are growing vegetables at home, check with any green fingered neighbours. It is also recommended that you undertake a soil acidity test. Kits can be bought inexpensively from garden centres and nurseries.

Ground levels

Be aware that a sloping plot will have different characteristics, for instance given the amount of sunlight it receives. Temperatures on a sloping plot can vary with low ground being particularly susceptible to frost.

Light and shade

Particularly in midsummer the amount of sunlight the plot receives will be a valuable tool when dealing with sensitive crops. Take note of any existing trees, canopies or structures that cast shadow onto your plot. Remember when planning your plot to place tall plantings and any crops grown on trellises on the north side of your plot to minimise shade throwing on lower growing crops.

Accessibility

Take a good look at the access on site. It is vital that you have good access when maintaining your plot, and you will need access areas wide enough to take a wheelbarrow. Also check that you have clear routes to the water supply, compost bins and sheds.

Leisure space

Try and find a draught free spot for refreshments or a quick 40 winks!

Soil testing

Drainage test

Time taken for water to drain:

_____

Assessment of soil

_____

_____

_____

Comments from other gardeners (if applicable)

_____

_____

_____

Ground levels

_____

_____

_____

Light and shade

Total areas of sunlight on plot: _____

Use the area below to make comments/drawings on the plot at different times of the day so that you can best assess what crops will thrive. Mark the hands on the clock, the plot is divided into hourly sections so you can mark where shadows fall and change throughout the day.

	08:00	
	10:00	
	12:00	
	14:00	
Observations:	16:00	
	18:00	

	08:00	
	10:00	
	12:00	
	14:00	
Observations:	16:00	
	18:00	

	08:00	
	10:00	
	12:00	
	14:00	
Observations:	16:00	
	18:00	

Whilst on site, it is also a good idea to make a rough sketch of how you would like your allotment to look. Remember to include access paths on your sketch, along with planting beds and any structures. Reference your sketch as the example below, and then use the page overleaf for a more accurate scale drawing when you return home.

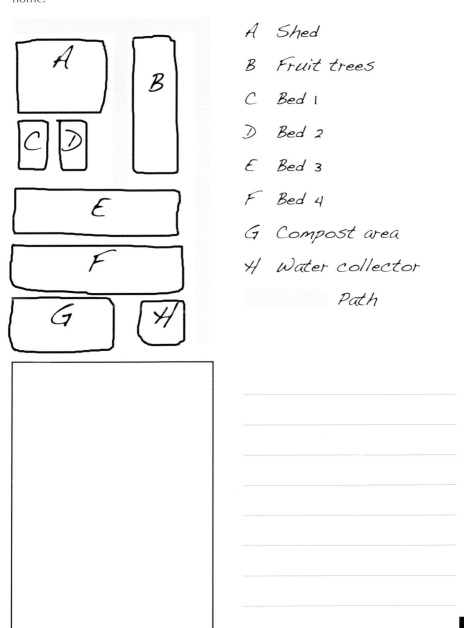

A   Shed

B   Fruit trees

C   Bed 1

D   Bed 2

E   Bed 3

F   Bed 4

G   Compost area

H   Water collector

       Path

Key:

Choosing your crops

Begin by making a wish list of the vegetables, fruits and herbs that you like most, and therefore would most like to grow. Don't forget to ask other members of the family what their preference would be. Remember that in the UK, climate will dictate to a certain extent your crops, particularly if you don't plan to have a greenhouse. You also need to be mindful that as well as different vegetable crops taking a varying quantity of nutrients from the soil, maximum yield per bed can be achieved by being aware of the harvest period. For instance, a spring sown crop of broad beans will probably finish cropping around mid summer and you can then plant "catch-up" crops such as lettuce or radishes in the area vacated by the broad beans.

It is also worth noting that you can have a constant supply of salad vegetables by sowing seeds in small batches in the spring and summer. Rather than fill one row with each vegetable, sow one row with a variety of vegetables, i.e 1/3 lettuce, 1/3 onions and 1/3 radishes. Two weeks later sow another row in the same way, then again after another two weeks etc. This will give you a steady supply of the vegetables, avoiding wastage, over a longer period. Sowing little and often you will enjoy a steady supply rather than a glut.

If you have completed light and shade assessment of your plot in the previous section, you should know the area and beds in your plot which will have limited sunlight, say 2 - 3 hours a day.

The following is a list of shade-tolerant vegetables and herbs to plant in semi-shaded areas:

Beetroot

Most often eaten cold in salads, adding a tasty splash of deep red colour, beetroot is easy to grow in most gardens. It can also be eaten hot, and there is a delicious recipes for Spicy Beetroot and coconut soup on page 75.

Broccoli

Part of the cabbage family of vegetables, there are many varieties of broccoli, the most popular of which is calabrese or green sprouting. Purple and white sprouting broccoli are however growing in popularity and have smaller shoots with a more intense flavour, though can be less hardy. All broccoli varieties should be picked while the flowers are still in bud, and if you plant different varieties you will have crops right through from early spring to late autumn. For a delicious broccoli recipe, see page 76.

Chives

A member of the onion family, chives are well worth cultivating in the vegetable and flower garden. They take up very little space, and the whole plant can be eaten from top to bottom - the bulbs as mild onions, the leaves in salads and flavouring, the flower heads as a splash of colour to salads. Try the recipe on page 77.

Garlic

Garlic was originally a native plant of many thousands of years ago. Evidence of it has been found in caves inhabited more than 10,000 years ago! Garlic is a key ingredient to a wide variety of recipes, and is quickly becoming regarded as a natural method to prevent heart disease and cancer. Growing garlic is well-suited to both the first time gardener and the more experienced - given the correct soil and planting time, common garlic is relatively maintenance free. Follow our easy recipe for alioli on page 77.

Kale

Packed with vitamins, kale is as delicious as it is nutritious and given that it is particularly hardy, it is a great crop for the first time gardener. Part of the cabbage family with deep green curly leaves, it has a long cropping season, is resistant to most pests and diseases and grows in almost any site and position. The recipe on page 77 is perfect served with traditional roast beef.

Kohlrabi

One of numerous members of the brassica family, a pale green or purple, bulb-shaped vegetable that tastes a bit like a mild turnip, and in fact can be substituted for turnip in most recipes. Increasingly popular, the mild, sweet flavour is delicious steamed or boiled, sliced and stir-fried (see page 78 for a tasty recipe) and added to stews or soups. It is more tolerant of warm weather than turnips and easier to grow successfully. It grows quickly, maturing in a few months from sowing.

Lettuce

This salad staple, with many varieties, is one of the first crops that the new vegetable gardener often attempts to grow, although they do require keen tending. Lettuce grows best in cool conditions and seed drills thrive in moist and shaded areas. Lettuce is great for harvesting all through the summer months.

Mint

There are many many varieties of mint which are easy to grow in both shade and sun and require very little maintenance, although they do not thrive in dry conditions. In fact, the problem with mint is that it can often grow too well and propagate throughout your garden.

Whilst peppermint (*Mentha piperita L.*) and spearmint (*Mentha spicata*) are the most popular, apple mint is also common - visit a herb garden or nursery which specializes in herbs to chose a selection for your own garden, as foliage, colour, fragrance and spread varies from one to another.

Follow our recipe for a delicious pea and mint soup on page 79

Parsley

Parsley does prefer sun, but will perform equally well in partial shade. Rich moist soil is the key and as parsley is biennial it will grow equally well in a pot on a windowsill. Curly parsley is often used as an attractive edging plant in flower gardens.

Radishes

They are an ideal vegetable for the amateur
gardener, or by way of introducing children to
growing vegetables as they are suited to most soil
types, rapidly reaching maturity and extremely
happy growing amongst taller vegetables. Radishes
like sun, but at the same time like cool conditions.

If they are grown in full sun during the summer,
they will run to seed or bolt very quickly. For this
reason they are ideally suited to as a growing
companion to other vegetables such as peas or
beans, which will provide them with natural partial
shade. You can also grow them in pots, enabling
you to move them around so they are not in full
sun.

For a different take on radishes, try our hot radish
recipe on page 80.

Rhubarb

Because rhubarb is so hardy and will survive
almost total neglect, it is often left to its own
devices in preference to other more demanding
vegetables.

If possible, it is preferable to grow rhubarb in full
sun, but as it is fairly tolerant of partial shade and
will remain in the same position for up to 10 years,
it is often to be found occupying the corner of a
vegetable patch. The soil immediately surrounding
the plant cannot be dug, so position it with this in
mind.

See page 80 for a delicious traditional rhubarb
crumble recipe.

Spinach

Spinach is a great vegetable for growing in cooler conditions. Young leaves can be washed and used in salads, older leaves should be cooked for a couple of minutes and served as a hot accompaniment. Spinach does not like the full heat of the summer sun, and thrives in shade. Whilst some gardeners feel spinach is hard to grow, choose varieties that are resistant to bolting and this will overcome most major problems. The ideal site is to plant them between rows of peas, beans or sweet corn. As these crops grow they will provide cover from the full sun in the warmer parts of the summer. Rotation is good, but not crucial for spinach. Try the delicious recipe on page 81.

Turnips

Turnips are a versatile crop, whose young tops can be used like spring greens, whilst the bulb is a delicious winter treat. Turnips like a steady supply of moisture, so should be watered regularly particularly in dry conditions. They are quick to mature and easy to grow and as such are a relatively trouble free crop. Your only chore will be selective thinning as too many plants will crowd quite quickly meaning decent roots will not develop. See page 83 for a tasty turnip recipe.

Spinach   *Turnips*

It's in the soil

If, as suggested in the previous section, you have taken a soil acidity test and found high levels of either acidity or alkalinity then the following pH preference list should be helpful. Generally, most vegetables prefer soil with a pH level between 6.5 and 7.0, but few gardeners are blessed with perfect soil and therefore have to adapt their plans to suit the soil they have.

Acid tolerant plants   (below pH 6.0)

Aubergine	5.5-6.8
Carrot	5.5-6.8
Celery	5.5-7.5
Endive	5.5-7.0
Garlic	5.5-7.5
Potato	5.8-6.5
Radish	5.5-6.5
Rhubarb	5.0-6.8
Sweet potato	5.5-6.5
Watermelon	5.5-7.0

Alkaline tolerant plants   (above pH 7.0)

Asparagus	6.5 - 7.5
Beetroot	6.5-7.5
Brussels sprouts	6.0-7.5
Cauliflower	6.0-7.5
Celery	5.5-7.5
Cucumber	6.0-7.5
Garlic	5.5-7.5
Leek	6.0-7.5
Melon	6.0-7.5
Okra	6.8-7.5
Onion	6.0-7.5
Shallot	6.5-7.5

Acid and Alkaline tolerant plants
Celery
Garlic

Soil, of course, can be enriched with fertilisers, and earthworms are the vegetable gardeners friend as they mix surface organic matter into the soil and their burrows bring air into the soil and also aid in drainage. You can encourage earthworms on to your plot by spreading compost on the surface of the soil.

Crop rotation

Crop rotation is the best known method for ensuring that your soil does not become bereft of the nutrients that your vegetables need to grow. The most practical rotation is a three-year rotation, and it is important to note that wherever possible each group should occupy the same amount of space to achieve the best results.

	Year 1	Year 2	Year 3
Bed 1	Roots	Others	Brassicas
	Do not add manure or lime; add a balanced fertiliser in spring,	Add a balanced fertiliser in spring.	Dig in manure or compost in autumn; add lime in spring.
Bed 2	Brassicas	Roots	Others
	Dig in manure or compost in autumn; add lime in spring.	Do not add manure or lime; add a balanced fertiliser in spring.	Add a balanced fertiliser in spring.
Bed 3	Others	Brassicas	Roots
	Add a balanced fertiliser in spring.	Dig in manure or compost in autumn; add lime in spring.	Do not add manure or lime; add a balanced fertiliser in spring.

Examples:

Roots	Potatoes, carrots, beetroot, parsnips
Others	Beans, lettuce, peas, celery, parsley family crops
Brassicas	Brussel sprouts, cabbage, cauliflower, plus swedes and turnips (which can also suffer from club-root disease)

Types of vegetable and herbs

Lettuce and greens

Many varieties of lettuce are suited to cooler climates, liking lots of rain and can be harder to cultivate in hot conditions. There are four basic types, cos (also called romaine), leaf (also called loose-leaf), crisphead, butterhead and stem (also called asparagus lettuce).

Positioning

Lettuce are not fussy about soil type as long as it is able to hold water. Their ideal is a soil which is well-drained and well-dug. Clay soil which has been broken down with lots of peat is excellent. Do not apply fertiliser or nutrient rich compost to the soil, this will cause rot. The key success factor with lettuce is to site them in a position which avoids the full blast of the sun in the middle of the day. Lettuces bolt if the weather becomes too hot or if there is a shortage of water.

Planting

Given that lettuce can have a relatively short shelf life after picking, sow frequently in small batches. Potted seedlings grow quickly and can be ready for transporting within 3 weeks. Some varieties of lettuce are more resistant to bolting than others. The varieties Fatima and Dolly (butterhead lettuce) are both slow to bolt. Because lettuce prefer cool conditions (great for the UK) they are ideal vegetables for growing near to other vegetables which crop at a different time, normally later. Plant lettuce where runner beans, broad beans, peas, brussels sprouts or sweet corn will provide them with shade in the hottest part of the day.

Care

If you do grow lettuce near taller vegetables, take care that they are not deprived of water. Lettuce need lots of water to mature quickly and larger crops may take the lion's share of moisture. If this is the case, water the lettuce well in dry conditions.

Harvesting and storage

Harvesting of baby lettuce leaves can begin about 2 weeks after setting out your transplants. Pick leaves from the outside and the plant will continue to produce leaves from the centre. In the latter part of the season pick the complete plant as you are unlikely to have more growth.

Ideally lettuce is best eaten just after picking, but if you are storing lettuce do not wash prior to storage. Store in a plastic bag, refrigerated.

Examples of lettuce and green varieties:

Crisphead lettuce	Batavian lettuce	Butterhead lettuce
Cos lettuce	Loose-leaf lettuce	Rocket
Endive	Chicory	Radicchio
Spinach	Swiss Chard	

Root crops

Beets, carrots, parsnips, radishes, turnips and potatoes are all commonly known as root crops. These vegetables offer a prolonged harvest season and, for the most part, a long storage life. They also produce a large amount of food in a small amount of space.

Positioning

Root crops grow best in well-drained, loose soil. Drainage is important because these crops are among the earliest planted and the latest harvested. If you have poor, clay soil, you might want to build a raised bed four to five inches high and 12 to 24 inches wide. Raised beds will help to reduce soil compaction, permit easier digging and will allow carrots and parsnips to attain greater length and be smoother in shape. Add sand and organic matter, such as manure, to heavy soils to improve drainage.

Planting

Root crops will not do well in a dry seedbed. The seedbed must be kept moist during the germination period. Therefore, you may need to sprinkle the bed with water every day until seeds have germinated.

Care

Some gardeners place a clear plastic sheet over the row after the seeds have been planted and watered. This warms the soil and conserves moisture. The sheet should be removed as soon as seedlings emerge. This procedure is especially useful for root crops such as carrots and parsnips which have a long germination period.

Harvesting and storage

For young beetroot greens for salads, cut about a month after sowing. Wash thoroughly with cold water to remove grit and dirt debris, then placed in a plastic bag in the fridge they will last up to say 10 days. These sweet leaves are delicious when sprinkled with balsamic vinegar. For baby beetroot, lift about 6 weeks after planting - full size beets should be 2-3 weeks later. Beetroots stored in a plastic bag will last up to 3 weeks if kept refrigerated.

Examples of root and stem vegetables:

Heirloom potatoes	New potatoes	Red potatoes
Russet potatoes	White potatoes	Yellow potatoes
Sweet potatoes	Carrots	Beetroot
Radishes	Parsnips	Turnips
Swedes	Salsify	Florence fennel

See pp 84 for a delicious parsnip recipe

The Onion family

Onion, or *Allium cepa*, is a cool weather vegetable that is easy to cultivate. Its scent belies the fact that it is a member of the lily family (and therefore toxic to many house pets). They are a staple ingredient in soups, salads, grills and sauces.

Positioning

Onions need a rich fertile, well-drained soil, so you may need to add nutrients to your soil to achieve the best results. Try adding about a cup of fertilizer for every 5-foot row of onions that you intend to plant. Dig in the fertilizer then cover with another 2 inches of soil. They are also intolerant to acid conditions, so after you have tested your soil, you may need to neutralize the acid by adding lime. An ideal site would be to make rows in the direction of the prevailing winds in your area. This will prevent moisture from sitting in the soil too long, which can cause disease.

Planting

When you should plant onions depends on where you live and how many hours of daylight you receive during the various seasons. You will also consider the types of onions that you are planting. Transplanted onion plants will produce the largest onions, provided that you care for them successfully. However, you can also buy grow onions from "sets". This is probably the simplest method and can even be used if you have a window box or indoor herb garden. They are specifically produced bulbs that are smaller and moister and are great if you want smaller baby onions. If you are going to get a set, your choices are usually limited to colour: yellow, white or red. Red are the sweetest, and yellow are the most pungent. If you are going to transplant your onions, you should ask at your local garden center which varieties are the hardiest in your area. If you are going to harvest green onions, place the larger of the sets within touching distance of each other. To produce dry (large, the kind you see at a grocery store) onions, place the transplants about 4 to 6 inches apart. Whichever type you are planting, set them 1 inch deep. Buy fresh seeds each year as they don't last from year to year.

Tip: you'll know you planted your onions too late in the season if they sprout a white onion flower, and this will result in a smaller bulb next year.

Care

Weeding needs to be done gently
by hand to avoid damaging the
tender roots of the plants, and you
should water little and often at
ground level. Excess water on the
foliage can cause disease. Apply more
fertilizer every 2 to 3 weeks after that.
Immediately water the soil once
you've put down the fertilizer. Pay
attention to the stems of the onion -
once it feels soft and looks a bit
droopy, you can stop using fertilizer.
This is also a sign that you will be
able to harvest your dry onions in
about 6 weeks.

Harvesting and storage

There is no "right" time to
harvest as you can begin pulling the
onions as soon as you feel they are
large enough for your needs. For
onions that store through the winter,
wait until the foliage turns yellow
and flops, then using a fork carefully
lift the bulbs and allow to dry
throughly. In dry conditions you can leave
the onions atop the soil to dry - but if you
have an area where you can place them off the
ground on a wire mesh this is preferable as the air can circulate around them, so
speeding the drying process. Once dried, they should be stored in a cool, dry area.
Try the pickling recipe on page 82.

Examples of the onion family:

Red onion	Pickling onion	Yellow onion
Shallot	Chives	Salad onion
Leeks	Garlic	

Cabbage family

There is a fair chance that a lot of the vegetables in your garden will be from the cabbage family, even if you are not a fan of cabbage itself. Many gardeners feel that eating home-grown produce from the cabbage family is a real revelation - the taste of this particular home-grown family is one of the best examples of why growing your own is best!

Positioning

The cabbage family need a rich, fertile soil to thrive in. You may want to dig in a green manure (page 62) to help maintain the soil and get the best out of your plants. They are a fairly hardly family, though not overly fond of very hot weather and will need regular watering.

Planting

Depending on the variety your plants will need to be spaced at least 18 inches apart, and again, depending on your choice of crop these will need planting through the year from spring to autumn.

Care

The cabbage family in particular can be prone to a variety of pests from flying insects to munching mammals. Provide as much protection as reasonable, and in the case of cauliflower and cabbage, covering with a horticultural fleece will help keep many of these at bay. In the case of tall growing plants you may need to provide stakes if your garden or plot is particularly exposed.

Another problem area with the cabbage family is club root. This is where the roots swell and become distorted. Plants are stunted and wilt in warm weather.

Favouring moist, warm acid soils, this disease creates spores as the roots rot which can lay dormant for many years and crops effected should be destroyed by burning to stop the disease spreading further.

Weeding should be kept under control by hand as this will stunt the growth of your crops.

Harvesting and storage

Harvest when the crop has reached the optimum size for your own personal use, and when the heads have become firm. Sprouts should be left on the stem of the plant until you want to use them, but if weather conditions turn harsh these can be picked and stored, unwashed, in a cool dry place.

The remainder of the cabbage family should be stored loosely, unwashed in a plastic bag in the fridge until required, though they will last no longer than a week.

Examples of the cabbage family:

Cabbage	Brussels sprouts	Broccoli
Broccoli rabe	Cauliflower	Kale
Kohlrabi		
Oriental greens (Pak Choi, Tatsoi etc)		

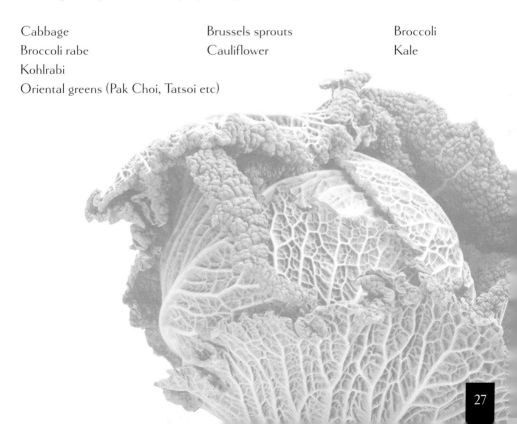

Peas and beans

Probably this family of crops is more evocative of a misspent youth on my grandfather's allotment than any other. Playing hide and seek amongst the supporting trellis then carrying back our harvest and sitting on the back door step shelling peas! Truely fresh peas and beans, picked straight from the plant, washed and cooked in minutes, tickle the tastebud like nothing else. Once you've tasted the incomparable sweetness of your first crop of peas, you'll be checking the vines daily for more. Beans are another surefire hit; this relatively easy group to cultivate will produce a bountiful harvest through until autumn. Beans and peas will have few problems provided they have a good basic healthy soil and they are kept well watered. Remove weak plants as and when these appear as these will be more prone to disease which could take hold on your crop.

Positioning

For best results incorporate moderate amounts of compost or well rotted manure deeply dug into the soil. Since peas and beans are shallow rooted plants they are sensitive to moisture fluctuations. Position rows for proper exposure to sunlight.

Planting

Work the soil when it is dry. Rake the soil to break it up and remove any debris. Form a 36" wide bed the length of your choice. Using a garden hoe form a shallow trench in the centre of the 36" wide bed about 4" deep. Additional rows should be 12" to 16" apart. Sow in spring after all danger of frost has passed, with the seeds about 2" apart and 1" deep. Push the seed into the soil to the depth of the first joint of your index finger or thumb, then water the bed gently without washing the seed out of the soil. Germination should occur within a week.

Keep the soil moist by lightly watering daily as this will help prevent the soil from crusting over, thereby allowing the seed to push through the surface easier. Thin the seedling to 3" and build your trellis within a week.

Cover the entire 36" wide bed with a light layer of straw to conserve moisture, attract worms, and reduce the growth of weeds in the beds.

Care

The roots of the crops are shallow, near the surface, so when pulling weed do not dig too deeply or root damage will result. If possible, remove any weeds that do appear by hand. You will also need to keep a close eye out for aphids and other pests. You can remove these by targeting the beasties with a gentle spray of water, but keep an eye on the level of pests that you encounter because you may need to take stronger measures.

Building a wigwam support trellis

Your crops will need supporting. Place bamboo canes loosely in the ground, in between your rows of seedlings, either side of the plants. Bring the two canes together over the top of the plant and tie together with string. Once tied together, press the canes slightly further into the soil for stability. Move along the row and place another set of canes about 3ft along, repeating the process until you have covered the length of your row. Next, place a cane between each of the "sets" that you created, resting on top of the "V" that has been created when you tied the canes. There should be no need to affix this top cane, but you can bind with string on the join if you prefer.

Harvesting and storage

All varieties of peas are ready for harvesting at slightly different times, but as a rule of thumb all pods should be picked before they loose their sheen. You will want to pick a pod and taste it to check that it is at the right stage. Green beans are ready to pick when they are about the size and length of a pencil. Anything larger than this will tend to be tough and/or stringy. Pods should be firm and full, free of defects. Remove the pod carefully to avoid damaging the vines. Hold the vine above the pod and pull off.

Examples of the pea and bean family:

Shelling peas	Mangetout	Snap peas
Asparagus peas	Climbing French bean	Broad bean
Dwarf French bean	Runner bean	Soya bean

Vine crops

Cucumbers, squash, melons and pumpkins are all members of the squash family - although they are very different vegetables. The plants are generally grown in mounds and send out vines that run over the ground. Some varieties come in bush or compact strains that don't require much space.

Positioning

Vine crops resist transplanting, so it's best to sow outdoors when all danger of frost has passed and the soil has warmed. If you need a head start, try starting seeds in fibre pots that will allow you to transplant without disturbing the seeds, or start early outdoors under protection. Remember to check plants every day to be sure they aren't getting too hot.

Planting

Prepare a slightly raised mound of soil 1-2 feet in diameter, leaving 3 feet (more for pumpkins and most winter squash) between mounds for the vines to run. Depending on your soil quality, it may be a good idea to dig in manure with the soil a few inches below ground level and then build the mound up on top of it. Space the plants evenly around the mound at least 6 inches apart.

Care

Vine crops need a lot of watering at ground level. Wherever possible you should avoid getting the foliage wet as this can lead to disease. If you are planning on growing a lot of vine crops you may want to invest in a drip irrigation system which will keep the soil moist. A mulch of hay between the mounds also helps to retain water, keep down weeds and keep fruit clean and dry.

Examples of vine crops:

Cucumber	Courgette	Marrow
Acorn squash	Banana squash	Butternut squash
Delicata squash	Hubbard squash	Kabocha squash
Spaghetti squash	Giant pumpkin	Mini pumpkin
Jack-o-lantern pumpkin	White pumpkin	Crenshaw melon
Honeydew melon	Muskmelon	Watermelon

Tomatoes

A word of caution concerning tomatoes. This ever popular crop in the garden has lured many a gardener into planting too many and being left with a surplus. Consider carefully what you want from your plant - are you looking for an early harvest, a sweet flavour or is being disease resistant important. There are many varieties from the tiny and popular cherry through to traditional salad and giant beefsteaks so pick carefully! You will need to decide wether your plot is most suited to vine or bush tomatoes. Vines are ideal for greenhouses but need a cane to support them and some tending to, whereas bush types are more compact and need less attention.

Positioning

Essential to a successful crop is keeping the soil moist - but not waterlogged - at all times. Regular feeding using a specialised tomato feed is also essential. Hardy varieties can be planted out, in a warm sunny sheltered position once all danger of frost has passed.

Planting

When the plants are 12–15cm (4–5in) tall, they are ready to be planted. Tomatoes are quite heavy feeders and will do best in a rich compost mix. Plant them up to the first pair of leaves, as this will encourage further roots to form on the lower stem. Water the compost with a fine, upturned rose on a watering can to gently firm down the surface on the compost, which should be sitting about 1cm (1/2 in) below the rim. Support taller-growing specimens by using a bamboo cane and twine.

Care

After 2-3 weeks, the plants should start flowering and you can begin to feed them. For the best flavour, you should aim to leave the fruits on the plants for as long as possible to ripen to their full deep colour.

Harvesting

Picking the crop regularly will encourage the plant to produce more. Bend back the fruit at the notch on the stem and gently twist it off, supporting the vine with your other hand. If you remove them with the green remains of the flower still attached it will prolong their shelf life.

Herbs

If you are growing your own home produce, then you really ought to have some basic herbs in your plot or pots (see chapter on pots and containers) as they often help bring out the best flavour in vegetables - just thinking of new potatoes or peas with fresh mint sets the mouth watering! Relatively easy to cultivate, herbs bring a bounty of fragrance, and whilst some like full sun, others are happy in the shade.

When choosing your herbs and planning your garden, pick those that like to be in the sun such as thyme, sage, rosemary, tarragon and oregano and those that like partial shade, such as sorrel, mustard, parsley and chervil.

Basil

There are over 150 varieties of basil. Sweet basil, (*L.Ocimum Basilcum*), comes from the mint family and is grown in warm, tropical climates - and as its name suggests, has a sweet, fragrant aroma. The name 'basil' derives from the Greek word for 'king' – and is considered by some to be the 'king of herbs'. Basil has literally been loved and hated in equal amounts all over the world! Considered as a sacred herb by the Hindus, considered in high esteem by the Indians and believed to be a symbol of love and fertility by the Romans, it was conversely loathed by the Greeks and in Europe during the Middle Ages, it was believed that scorpions bred under pots of growing basil – so just smelling a basil plant could result in the unsuspecting 'sniffer' forming a scorpion in the brain! Native to Africa, India and Asia, this spicy herb, with anise-like undertones and an aroma of cloves, has a long and controversial history. As probably the most commonly-known variety of basil, being traditionally associated with Italian cuisine, sweet basil is a culinary classic used to flavour tomato-based soups and sauces, pasta and rice dishes, meats, vegetables, cheese dishes and green salads.

Chervil

From the plant 'Anthriscus cerefolium', chervil is a classic ingredient in the French herb blend 'Fines Herbes'. Originally native to southern Russia, this light green, fern-like-leaf herb was transported by the Romans to France, where it became, and remains, a staple herb in French cuisine. Chervil is familiar to Easter celebrations in parts of Europe, because its aroma is similar to that of myrrh and its spring-time growth is a symbol of renewal and regeneration.

Sometimes known as 'gourmet parsley', chervil is an aromatic and sweet herb, with a delicate hint of liquorice. Chervil is used to flavour soups, stews, salads, omelettes, fish, poultry, creamy sauces, new potatoes, baby vegetables and cheeses. Chervil is the herb which gives Béarnaise sauce its distinctive taste.

Coriander

Despite it's name in Greek, ('koris'), translating as 'bed bug', coriander, the seed of the 'Coriandrum sativum' is probably the one of the world's most widely used and popular herbs – and possibly the oldest, dating back to at least the second millennium BC. Traditionally used in Middle Eastern, Asian, Oriental and Latin American cuisine, this highly aromatic, annual herb belongs to the parsley family. Its recognition in European cuisine hasincreased over the last few decades and shows no decline. The whole of the plant is edible, but the leaves and the dried seeds are most commonly used in cooking. The leaves, known as cilantro, are earthy and quite pungent, mostly used in savoury dishes, such as soups, curries, stuffings, breads, chutneys, salads and as a popular garnish. The dried coriander seeds have a distinctly different citrus-like taste and can either be used whole or ground for culinary use. Coriander seeds are used in savoury dishes such as meats, curries, seafood, sausages, chutneys, casseroles and soups – but they can also be used in sweet dishes, such as desserts, pies and pastries.

Dill

Deriving from the perennial herb, 'Anethum graveolens', the seeds of the plant, known as dill seeds, are used as a spice; and the fresh leaves, known as dill weed, are used as a herb. Fresh green in colour and providing a refreshing and mild flavour, dill is an ancient herb, originating in Europe and Asia, (as far back as the Bible). Dill, which comes from the Norse word 'dilla', means to soothe, or lull. In ancient medicine it was used to soothe the stomach after meals, relieving bloating and gas – and for colic in babies. In ancient Greece it was considered a sign of wealth and in Middle Age Europe, dill was believed to protect against the evils

Dill/cont.

of witchcraft. Dill is a popular addition to German, Scandinavian and Russian dishes, with the flavour of the leaves and seeds providing very different flavourings to recipes – for this reason they are not interchangeable with each other. The leaves (weed) are fragrant, with a clean, delicate and simple taste, good for flavouring foods such as fish, shellfish, soups, cream sauces, mild cheeses, potato dishes, vegetables, (particularly cucumber), and dips. The seeds have a spicier, more potent flavour – similar to the caraway seed and anise and can be used whole or ground. Dill seeds are an excellent addition to food when sprinkled in or over casseroles, stews, soups, salads, rice dishes, root vegetables and salad dressings.

Mint

The mint plant, (Mentha) has literally hundreds of different varieties, the most significant of which being peppermint (*Mentha piperita L.*) and spearmint (*Mentha spicata*). This fast-growing plant, native to Asia, is a popular culinary herb, with variable coloured leaves ranging from dark green to purple, to pale yellow. Used by the Romans to whiten teeth, it was also believed to symbolise hospitality.

Beneficial to gardens, the aromatic leaves repel unwanted insects and attract useful insects. With a fresh, sweet flavour and a cool aftertaste, the leaves, (dried or fresh), are the culinary source of the plant.

Mint has a plethora of culinary uses including teas, jellies, sauces, syrups, candy, ice cream, beverages, even alcohol - such as crème de menthe. Mint is a popular complement to lamb dishes in the UK.

Oregano

Mediterranean Oregano (*Origanum vulgare L.*) translated into Greek means 'Joy of the mountains'. Used prolifically in Greece, Italy and in Italian-American cuisine, this pungent herb produces a number of varieties, specific to where the plant is cultivated. Oregano is a relation of marjoram and produces a warm, slightly bitter taste. It is a classic ingredient in the herb blend, 'Bouquet Garni'. The leaves are used as a culinary ingredient and surprisingly, the dried herb is more flavourful than the fresh herb itself. Oregano is popularly used in Italian cuisine to add flavour to tomato sauces, pizzas, salad dressings and vegetables. It is also a staple in Greek cuisine, traditionally cooked with lamb and Greek salad. Oregano complements dishes with lemon and garlic and is a flavour-rich addition to red meats, fish, pork, chicken, Moussaka and hot, spicy dishes.

Parsley

Parsley (*Petroselinum crispum*) is one of the more well-known and popular herbs. It has a number of varieties, the most common being the flat leafed Italian parsley and curly parsley. The two have distinctly different tastes, so are attributed in different ways for culinary use, e.g. curly parsley is commonly used as a garnish, whereas flat leaf parsley has a stronger, more pungent flavour. As an ancient herb, parsley has an eventful history. The Greeks used parsley to crown their 'victors' at their games events and the Romans believed that wearing a wreath made of parsley would prevent inebriation, by absorbing the alcoholic fumes. Parsley also has historical links to the occult. Parsley is a versatile herb, with a mild, fresh aroma and a slightly peppery, but not overpowering, taste. Popular in Central and Eastern Europe and West Asia, fresh, chopped parsley is often sprinkled over dishes for extra taste. Parsley is a congenial flavouring for a broad range of dishes, such as potato dishes, vegetables, rice, fish, soups, chicken, lamb, steaks, stews, green salads, dips, sauces, stocks, omelettes and butters. It is also part of the French herb blends 'fines herbes' and 'Bouquet Garni'.

Rosemary

Native to the Mediterranean and a member of the mint family, rosemary, from the Latin 'Rosmarinus' , translates into English as 'Dew of the Sea' – due to the complementary conditions for its growth by the coast. The herb comes from the small evergreen shrub, *Rosmarinus officinalis*.Legend has it that the Virgin Mary, fleeing from Herod, draped her blue

Rosemary/cont.

cloak on a rosemary bush, laying a white flower on top. In the morning the flower had turned blue, as a consequence the bush was then dubbed the 'Rose of Mary'.

In ancient Greece it was believed that rosemary strengthened the function of the brain and revitalized the memory, so much so that students wore springs of rosemary in their hair during examinations. Rosemary was also associated with remembrance, due to its enhancement of the memory and was often worn and/or burned at funerals and weddings. Rosemary has a slightly astringent, pine-like taste with an aromatic fragrance. The flavour is best retained as whole 'needles'. Used predominantly in Mediterranean cuisine, rosemary complements dishes such as roasted meats, (traditionally used with lamb), poultry, stews, tomato sauces, marinades, roasted vegetables and potatoes, soups and fish.

Sage

Sage, the Latin 'salveo' meaning 'to save' is a well-known herb from the evergreen shrub '*Salvia officinalis*'. An established member of the mint family, there are a few hundred different types of sage. The most commonly used variety being silvery-grey in colour and sporting a strong, slightly musky aroma and a pine-like, woody flavour. Dating back as far as ancient Rome, the Romans heralded sage as a sacred herb, which was used during planting and harvesting ceremonies for prosperity and good luck. In folklore, sage was a symbol of wisdom, enhanced memory, longevity and virtue – hence the term 'an old sage', meaning an old, wise person. Sage is famous for its culinary contribution to sage and onion stuffing, used for poultry dishes, but it is also a savoury complement to pork, veal, sausages, potatoes, seafood, soups, stews, savoury scones and muffins and even speciality cheeses and teas. The chopped leaves are an excellent addition to salads, chutneys and pickles and work as an attractive garnish for soups and stews.

Tarragon

Known also as the 'dragon herb', from the small shrub '*Artemisia dracunculus L.*', tarragon is part of the sunflower family. The origin of the name, tarragon, is somewhat ambiguous, but is possibly a play on the French word 'estragon', which means 'little dragon', believed to be named so due to the plant's roots curling,

like a dragon's tail. There are two varieties of tarragon cultivated, French and Russian, however the most commercially used tarragon comes from the dried leaves of the French tarragon plant. Native to Russia and Western Asia, tarragon was used in the Middle Ages to treat dog bites and as an antidote for poisonous snake bites. Tarragon is a healthy green colour, with a bittersweet, peppery flavour and a slight aroma and taste of anise. It is traditionally associated with vinegar and fish dishes.

Popular in French cuisine, tarragon is one of the traditional ingredients in the French herb blend 'Fines Herbes' – and a main ingredient in Béarnaise sauce. It is also a complementary flavouring when used in vinegars, dressings, pickles, relishes, mustards, cream sauces, sour cream, yoghurt and butters, as well as an accompaniment for dishes such as fish, meat, seafood, chicken, soups and stews, vegetables, tomato, cheese and egg dishes. In parts of Eastern Europe, tarragon is added to carbonated soft drinks as a refreshing beverage.

Thyme

Thyme *'Thymus vulgaris'* was a symbol of courage in ancient Greece and Roman soldiers bathed in an infusion containing thyme, to bring courage, invigoration and strength. Indigenous to the Mediterranean, this tiny-leafed herb with grey-green leaves is a member of the mint family and is cultivated in several different varieties. Regular thyme is most popularly marketed and sold, but for a different taste try using lemon thyme for a zesty kick. The leaves are dried, then chopped or ground for culinary use, providing a subtle and fresh aroma, with a slight hint of mint to its taste. A versatile and much-used herb, thyme is an essential ingredient in the French herb blend, 'Bouquet Garni'. Thyme's taste complements most meats, soups, sauces, vegetables, stews, pasta sauces, poultry, seafood, chowders, eggs and tomato-based dishes.

Guide to vegetable yields

As a guide, if you plant the following crops in a 1m (3ft) row, you can expect the following approximate yields:-

Bean, runner	6kg (13lb)
Bean, French	1.5kg (3lb)
Beetroot	2.5kg (5lb)
Broccoli	1kg (2lb)
Brussels sprouts	2kg (4 1/2lb)
Cabbage	3.2kg (7lb)
Carrot	3.2kg (7lb)
Cauliflower	2kg (4 1/2lb)
Celery	1.5kg (3lb)
Chinese cabbage	1.5kg (3lb)
Courgette	3kg (6 1/2lb)
Leek	3kg (6 1/2lb)
Lettuce	1kg (2lb)
Onion, bulb	2.5kg (5lb)
Parsnip	3.2kg (7lb)
Pea	2kg (4 1/2lb)
Potato	4kg (9lb)
Salad onion	340g (12oz)
Squash	4kg (9lb)
Spinach	1kg (2lb)
Swede	2kg (4 1/2lb)
Sweetcorn	1kg (2lb)
Tomato	3.2kg (7lb)
Turnip	2kg (4 1/2lb

Guide to harvest times

This is the average length of time you will need to allow between sowing seeds and harvesting your vegetables.

Short-term crop

Asparagus pea	8-10 weeks
Bean, French	8-12 weeks
Bean, runner	12-14 weeks
Beetroot	12-16 weeks
Broccoli	12-16 weeks
Cabbage, chinese (oriental greens)	10-14 weeks
Carrot (early)	12-16 weeks
Courgette and marrow	10-14 weeks
Cucumber	12-14 weeks
Fennel	10-14 weeks
Kohlrabi	8-12 weeks
Lettuce	6-14 weeks
Okra	16 weeks
Potato (early)	12-16 weeks
Radish	3-12 weeks
Salad Onion	10 weeks
Spinach	8-14 weeks
Sweetcorn	14 weeks
Swish chard	12 weeks
Tomato	16 weeks
Turnip	6-12 weeks

Medium-term crop

Aubergine	20 weeks
Bean, broad	14-26 weeks
Carrot	16-20 weeks
Cabbage, summer and autumn	20-26 weeks
Cauliflower, summer	20-26 weeks
Celery	18-30 weeks
Herbs	12-18 weeks
Pea	12-32 weeks
Peppers	18 weeks
Potato	20-22 weeks

Medium-term crop

Potato, sweet	18-24 weeks
Pumpkin and winter squashes	10-18 weeks
Salsify	25 weeks
Shallot	18-26 weeks
Swede	20-24 weeks

Long-term crop

Artichoke, globe	8 months
Artichoke, Jerusalem	40-50 weeks
Asparagus	12 months
Broccoli, sprouting	40 weeks
Brussels sprouts	28-36 weeks
Cabbage, spring	30-36 weeks
Cauliflower, spring	40-46 weeks
Celeriac	30-36 weeks
Garlic	24-30 weeks
Horseradish	28-30 weeks
Kale	30-36 weeks
Leek	30-46 weeks
Onion, bulb	22-46 weeks
Parsnip	34 weeks
Rhubarb	15 months

If time or space restricts you from raising your own seeds, it is possible to buy young plants for transplanting to your plot from garden centres and nurseries. If you are buying bare root plants, ensure that the roots have been carefully wrapped to prevent them from drying whilst you transport them home.

Also, be aware that it is generally always preferable to raise your own seeds for any vegetable in the cabbage family, as bought transplants can import incurable club-root disease into your garden which can wreck your harvest.

Sowing

In general terms sowing seeds is very easy once you get the hang of it. Remember to follow the instructions on the packet and space seeds evenly. Some find it easier to tip the seeds into the palm of the hand and take pinches of the seed to sprinkle along the trough. You can also fold the seed packet to create a funnel and tap the packet gently to release the seeds.

Certain vegetables will benefit from being sown under protective cover, i.e a cloche, or in a greenhouse, which will then need transplanting at a later date as young plants. Growing seeds in a greenhouse will give the plants a good start, and in cooler regions it will enable earlier harvesting. Sowing in containers under cover will provide the best conditions for germination.

Aubergines
When to sow seeds   Early to mid spring, under cover
When to transplant   Early to mid summer, after all danger of frosts

Broccoli
When to sow seeds   Early spring through to summer
When to transplant   Mid spring and late summer

Brussel sprouts
When to sow seeds   Early to mid summer
When to transplant   Mid to late summer

Broad beans
When to sow seeds   Mid to late spring, under cover
When to transplant   Early summer, after all danger of frosts

Cabbage
When to sow seeds   Early spring to mid summer
When to transplant   Mid spring to late summer

Cauliflower
When to sow seeds   Early spring to early summer
When to transplant   Mid spring to mid summer

Celeriac

When to sow seeds	Early spring
When to transplant	Mid to late spring

Celery

When to sow seeds	Late winter to early spring
When to transplant	Mid to late spring

Climbing beans

When to sow seeds	Mid to late spring, under cover
When to transplant	Late spring to summer, after all danger of frosts

Courgettes & marrows

When to sow seeds	Mid spring, under cover
When to transplant	After all danger of frosts

Cucumbers

When to sow seeds	Early to mid spring, under cover
When to transplant	After all danger of frosts, spring in greenhouses

Florence fennel

When to sow seeds	Early spring, under cover
When to transplant	Mid spring

Kale

When to sow seeds	Mid spring to mid summer
When to transplant	Early to late summer

Kohlrabi

When to sow seeds	Early to mid spring
When to transplant	Mid to late spring

Leeks

When to sow seeds	Late winter to early spring
When to transplant	Late spring to early summer

Lettuce

When to sow seeds   Late winter to early spring, under cover
When to transplant   Mid spring

Melons

When to sow seeds   Mid spring, under cover
When to transplant   Late spring to early summer, after all danger of frosts

Okra

When to sow seeds   Early to mid spring, under cover
When to transplant   Early to mid summer, after all danger of frosts

Onions

When to sow seeds   Mid to late winter, under cover
When to transplant   Spring or autumn

Peppers

When to sow seeds   Early spring, under cover
When to transplant   Late spring

Potatoes

See overleaf

Pumpkins & winter squash

When to sow seeds   Mid spring, under cover
When to transplant   After all danger of frosts

Sweetcorn

When to sow seeds   Mid spring, under cover
When to transplant   After all danger of frosts

Tomatoes

When to sow seeds   Early to mid spring, under cover
When to transplant   Mid to late spring and early summer

Potatoes

Potatoes are grown from seed potatoes and your crop will be better if the potatoes are "chitted" prior to planting.

To do this, stand the seed potatoes in a shallow tray (or reuse the base from an egg box) with the end with the largest amount of eyes facing upwards. Store them in a dry cool place, but make sure the temperature is not so low as to frost.

To plant the potatoes dig a trench about 10cm deep by 10cm wide and put the potatoes in the trench about 30cm apart. Cover the potatoes with about 3cm of soil.

Plant the early varieties early to mid spring and the the main crop mid to late spring. Ensure soil is kept moist but avoid overwatering. You will need to purchase your seed potatoes from farm shops or garden centres as most supermarket potatoes have been treated to inhibit sprouting.

Pots and containers

If space is limited, or growing your own produce is something that you would love to do without it being too big a drain on your time and other resources, then an ideal place to start is with grow bags and containers. Containers and grow bags are also ideal for getting children interested in growing produce.

Grow bags

If you say "grow bags" to most gardeners, they first thing that springs to mind is tomatoes or strawberries, but these little treasures are actually a great way of growing shallow root vegetables - particularly aubergines, chillies and cucumber - in a manageable way. They are also potentially less likely to be infected by any soil-borne diseases and will thrive in a sunny spot with a little TLC!

Traditional grow bags measure 35cm x 95cm (13in x 37in) and are big enough for three vegetable plants that will provide you with enough food for several meals.

Ideally you should plant two to three plants in each bag during spring for a summer harvest, following these basic instructions:-

1. Place the bag in the position you have chosen - wherever possible this should be against a south facing wall or fence which will act as a sun trap, and protect the crops from high winds. Loosen the compost in the bag by shaking gently, but thoroughly, and kneading with your hands to break up any large clumps.

2. Pierce the bottom of the bag, for drainage, and cut out the marked planting squares. If you are planting rows of salads, cut out a long rectangle.

3. Scoop out the compost from each square leaving a hole big enough for the root ball of your plant, obviously ensuring that you leave enough compost underneath the root. Put a plant in each hole and refill around it with the compost, compacting the compost gently. The top of each root ball should be just below the top of the bag. Water well and label.

You may also, depending on your chosen crop, need to provide a growing frame for your plants - bamboo canes are a cheap and traditional option, but there are also agricultural frame sets available now specifically for grow bags.

It is also possible, and indeed in some instances preferable, to make your own grow bag - particularly if you use bags with handles, such as the heavy duty "bag for life" carrier bags. Essentially you need a sturdy plastic bag, which you then need to fill with growing medium, and then follow the basic planting instructions as above. It is also possible to hang bags on a sturdy support wall which would make them perfect height for anyone who has a difficult time reaching the ground to garden. The bags can be moved during the season as well, if you find that there is a change in your garden plans. This type of hanging grow bag is particularly suited for growing fragrant herbs near the door back into your house - plant half a dozen or so different herbs on a trellis to create your own bouquet garni!

What to grow

As mentioned, grow bags are ideally suited to plants that don't have deep roots, such as tomatoes, cucumbers, sweet peppers, chilli peppers, aubergines and courgettes. Endive, lettuce, basil and rocket are also a popular grow bag crop.

Aftercare

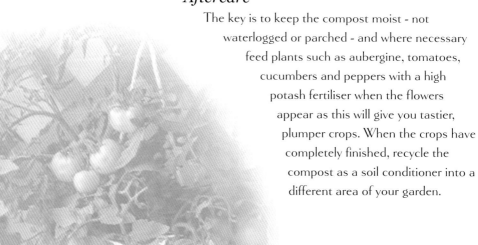

The key is to keep the compost moist - not waterlogged or parched - and where necessary feed plants such as aubergine, tomatoes, cucumbers and peppers with a high potash fertiliser when the flowers appear as this will give you tastier, plumper crops. When the crops have completely finished, recycle the compost as a soil conditioner into a different area of your garden.

Containers

Containers for your vegetables can be just about anything. Plastic pots and troughs can be bought very cheaply and look attractive. Ceramic pots are going to cost more but they look better. If you want you can use nearly anything. Some supermarkets sell off the buckets cut flowers are delivered in very cheaply. These are a perfect medium for all kinds of vegetables. Drill a few holes in the bottom and you have a nice large pot.

Containers which are purpose-made, such as potato barrels, are available in different sizes – a good average one is 44cm/17 in in diameter with an 80 ltr/17 gallon capacity which is enough to provide a fair-sized crop. Heat retentive polypropylene constructions keeps the compost warm encouraging healthy growth when our summers are letting the side down!

Strawberry pots have been around for quite some time and this is another good way to provide yourself with home grown fare. Your can reap a good crop of strawberries out of these pots in one season.

Raised beds

More and more people are constructing their own containers these days – by way of raised beds. These are basically wooden planks or boards nailed or screwed together into an oblong or square, placed on top of existing soil, possibly not really good quality, and filled up with really good compost. If you construct one or two or even more of these, leave a space between them, so that you will have the ability to move around to all sides for planting, weeding and hopefully, harvesting without stepping on the soil and thus compacting it.

Compost, fertilizer and water

You're going to be asking a lot from your pots so you really need to start with a decent compost. Go to your local garden centre or gardener's supply store, find someone who knows what they are about and buy the best for the job of growing vegetables. Next you are going to need to feed the plants. You can feed with a liquid feed as you water or make life simple and use a slow release fertiliser such as Osmacote added to the compost before you plant up.

Your biggest problem is going to be watering. The more containers you have the larger the job of watering.

Watering has been simplified in recent years with the introduction of a drip watering systems.

You can get sophisticated systems - computer controlled watering systems - or just a very simple system from hardware stores for not a lot of money – a small price to pay for well watered veggies!

Of course, you could get caught by a hosepipe ban, but if you invest in a water butt you can get low pressure watering kits or pumps, to provide mains-like pressure from your water butt. Using these, even when there is a hosepipe ban on, is perfectly legal. It's your water!

It is also a good idea to use moisture retaining granules, again available from most nurseries and garden centres, because these will cut down on the amount of watering you will need to do. After planting it is also a good idea to cover the surface of the compost with gravel or bark mulch as this will help retain moisture.

Starting off your edible containers

The most important thing to remember when attempting to grow vegetables in containers, is the size of the container plus the amount and quality of the soil in relation to the crop. For example, 8 – 10 ltr/3 cu ft of soil is a good rule for many vegetables. The water and nutrients necessary for the healthy growth of the plant will only be supplied satisfactorily in an amount of around this size.

Slow-release fertilizers offer many advantages when growing vegetables in pots. They avoid the common "feast-or-famine" syndrome that occurs when standard fertilizers are applied inconsistently. With standard fertilizers roots are briefly surrounded by plenty of nutrients, but these soon wash away again leaving roots to starve. Likewise, fast-release fertilizers are easy to apply in excess consequently damaging the plant. Slow-release fertilizers hand out their nutrients gradually and therefore potential problems are minimized.

Crops for your pots!

Tomatoes

Probably the most popular patio vegetable is the tomato, grown for many years in this country for its delightful varied fruits but also from the decorative aspect and its delightful smell.

There are special varieties which are suited to small patios — small fruited or sweet red cherry- sized tomatoes. 'Tiny Tim' and 'Gardener's delight' are good examples of this type. Also available are yellow or plum-shaped fruits of standard size such as the bush tomato 'Golden Boy' which is particularly suited to container gardening.

Another tomato well-suited to small spaces and baskets is the variety 'Tumbler' which produces lots of cascades of small tomatoes. The hanging basket is the perfect medium for this plant and will result in a beautiful picture of lots of tiny fruit in various colours trailing over the sides.

Tall-growing tomatoes do just as well in containers — maybe you will need to consider the size of the container if it is a particularly large plant like "Beefsteak", for example. Remember to pinch the side shoots out in these larger varieties. These are the little shoots that grow between the stem of the plant and the main leaves. Left in, the plant will concentrate on throwing out more leaves than fruit and you'll get a smaller yield. Sometimes you will feel quite mean removing them particularly when they have been left for a while and have grown quite large as you will think it is part of the plant. You will be rewarded by a bigger crop if you keep on top of this job. Don't pinch out shoots which have no leaves — these are the ones on which the tomatoes will grow. Place them in a nice sunny spot, water well and fertilize very regularly with a tomato fertilizer and your harvest should be a bumper one no matter which varieties you choose.

Lettuce

Lettuce is generally a cool season crop, but a few types will do reasonably well even in warmer weather with proper care. Introduction of new, improved types is happening every year, and there are hundreds of individual lettuces with various cold and heat tolerances. They are all able to be grown in containers quite easily as they have fairly shallow roots.

Loosehead

With a variety of colours, textures, flavours, and leaf shapes, there is a place for loosehead lettuces in every garden. Plant loosehead lettuce, as opposed to the tightly formed firmer varieties, which take much longer to form, because with these you are able to 'cut and come again'. Just break off as much as you need from the outer leaves at the base without disturbing the roots so that new leaves will grow continuously. Harvest can start as soon as the leaves are big enough to eat, and most plants will regenerate leaves as quickly as you harvest them.

Romaine

Other names for this lettuce are Cos, Roman, and Manchester lettuce. Romaine is a nutritious deep green, long-leaved, mildly bitter lettuce with crisp mid ribs. It requires a long growing season and bolts readily.

Lollo Rosso and Salad Bowl

These varieties are well-suited to this kind of harvesting also. Grow them from seed in a tub or box planting in April or May. Thin them out until they are about 15cm/6in apart. You will have a good supply of fresh, tasty salad leaves from summer to early autumn.

Although lettuces differ widely in form and in growing season requirements, they all share the same gardening basics. Loose, rich, well-drained soil, mulch, and a minimum of half a day of sun are absolute musts for the best results. Good growth is the goal, and continuous moisture is the key. For an earlier crop, start seeds indoors or buy young plants as soon as they are available in the garden centre. The seeds are small, so put a few in each starting container lightly with soil, and when the seedlings have sprouted, be sure to harden off the plants by exposing them to the cold little by little for a couple of weeks before transplanting into the garden. Use bolt resistant varieties that mature quickly for best results in containers.

Courgettes, Peppers & Aubergines

If you are growing tomatoes in a south-facing area you can place courgettes, peppers and aubergines alongside them in tubs or boxes. They all need plenty of sun and do very well in containers with plenty of water and fertilizer.

Runner beans

Beans are perfect for a sunny, sheltered spot. They do well growing in moist, fertile soil in a sheltered spot away from strong winds, but can also be grown successfully in pots in the correct compost. If you are growing beans in containers, choose pots at least 45cm/18in in diameter and make sure there are plenty of drainage holes. Fill with a mixture of equal parts loam-based compost and loam-free compost. Sowing seeds indoors gives a faster and more reliable germination rate, particularly for runner beans. At the end of spring sow a single bean seed, 4cm/1.5in deep, in a 7.5cm/3in pot filled with multi-purpose compost.

Water well, label and place on a sunny windowsill to germinate. Seedlings will be ready to plant out after about three weeks.

Put in a cold frame or a cool porch prior to planting out for a few days so that they can cope with the conditions outside.

Before planting in the containers you have ready for them, create supports for both climbing French and runner beans.

Either make a wigwam with 2.4m/8ft canes, lashed together with string at the top, or create a parallel row of canes, which have their tops tightly secured to a horizontal cane. Each row should be 60cm/23in apart and canes spaced 15cm/6in apart in the row.

Dwarf and climbing French beans

Most have small, round pods, although as with every rule there are exceptions. When the weather is changeable, or very hot, making the growing conditions difficult, climbing French beans will often crop better than runner beans.

Because French beans are self-fertile they do not need any pollinating insects present to ensure a good crop. Being self-fertile also means they can be grown early and late in the season under cover, enabling you to extend the picking season.

Climbing French beans grow well in the ground and containers. Many have decorative flowers and coloured pods, and tend to be a little less vigorous, so they do not need quite as long support wires or canes as for the runner beans described above.

Sow bean seeds in small pots in multi-purpose compost as for runner beans. Push one or two beans into each pot. The pots can then placed in a heated greenhouse at a minimum temperature of 10-15C (50-60F) and grown on in the greenhouse, if possible, or otherwise window ledge or garden shed before moving to a cold frame to gradually harden off prior to planting out into containers.

Climbing and dwarf French beans are a good source of vitamin A and K, and many gardeners and cooks believe French beans are better used for freezing than runner beans and like their climbing cousins, are also self fertile, making them ideal for growing under cover early or up to late in the season. Being dwarf, normally only growing 30 to 40cm/12-16in tall they need no supports, which makes them ideal for growing in patio containers.

Like the climbing types, the pods come in a variety of colours all offering different tastes and textures whether eaten freshly picked or taken out of the freezer and cooked.

Cucumbers

Growing cucumbers can be fun but they do need somewhere where there is little sun, and which is sheltered from the wind.

It is best to grow cucumbers yourself from seed starting them off ona window ledge or similar, preferably over a radiator. Sow them in small pots and plant them out in early summer.

It is important to choose the right variety which should be all-female and mildew-resistant.

Fruits are formed on all-female plants without pollination by insects.

Bella' is a good variety – with long fruits – and 'Paska' with short fruits.
Be ready to support the plants with trellis or poles, and start to tie them up quite firmly when the fruit starts to form, since they become quite heavy.

Do your homework!

Leeks, spring onions, shallots, beetroot, carrots and many other vegetables can all be successfully grown in containers and raised beds – the choices are endless.

So if it's something you enjoy, there are plenty of resources out there for you to have a plentiful kitchen garden. After all, the pleasure of harvesting your own veggies and taking them straight to the kitchen to cook is immeasurable, not to mention delicious!

Herbs in pots

Herbs historically have been always used for preserving and flavouring food, as well as making medicines and toiletries. There are some outstanding ornamental herb gardens around at larger country houses, as the aesthetic appeal has always been important, as to the same degree, has their ornamental qualities. There is nothing as satisfying as picking fresh herbs almost all year round and using them straight away. They combine the delights of a flower garden with the productivity of a regular vegetable garden. They take very little looking after and it doesn't take much to start it off. The results can be decorative, excellent in aroma and flavour, and cheap to grow.

Containers

If you are a user of fresh herbs and don't have a large enough garden for growing herbs, you should try to have at least one large container, or plastic window box which is ideal for growing herbs. Whichever container you pick, make sure it has drainage holes in the bottom. Most species of herbs are vulnerable to water logging, so as a general rule you should start off with a layer of broken crocks or gravel at the bottom of the container.

They do better in boxes and trays etc. than in the actual vegetable garden as they can be treated differently from surrounding larger plants.

They are also portable which has its advantages. For example, they need a lot less feeding and not as much water as regular vegetables or flowers. However, remember that they will be in containers, which can dry out quickly so they must be watered on regular basis, and have a good layer of chards at the base of the soil for good drainage.

Planting

The amount of nutrients contained in proprietary compost at the first planting should be sufficient for them. Perennials will need a fresh supply of nutrients every spring. Most perennials tend to lose their leaves in autumn but they will re-shoot in spring if properly taken care of.

Of the perennials, lavender, rosemary and thyme stay green in winter. There are basically two kinds of herbs, some which need a lot of moisture and some that don't. Herbs that prefer moisture-rich soil include basil, cilantro, tarragon, and parsley, while herbs that don't need as much water, or "Mediterranean herbs," include chives, oregano, sage, rosemary, thyme, bay, marjoram, and lavender.

A good idea is to plant moisture-loving herbs in plastic containers which retain water, and put Mediterranean herbs in terra cotta containers, if possible, which draw out the water. No matter what kind of container you use you must make sure there it has drainage holes at the bottom. This is very important, otherwise, plants can rot from sitting in water.

Watering

Plant herbs with the same moisture needs together. For variety, try a tall, medium, and cascading plant together in the same pot. How much water depends on weather, soil, sun exposure, Don't leave any of the little plants bought from nurseries in their little plastic containers for very long as they will dry out very quickly.

Moisture-loving herbs in a sunny window will need watering twice a week – put them on a kitchen window ledge and you will see them every day and hopefully remember to do this. If kept outside in the sun, water once or twice a week—or every 10 to 12 days for herbs that like drier conditions.

Care & Harvesting

Herbs can be planted on their own or in combination with other herbs. When planting more than one variety in a container, care should be taken that there will be ample growing space for all the plants. Prune the faster growing varieties regularly to ensure they do not overgrow their slower companions. Also, competition for space and nutrients will result in some varieties flourishing while others will suffer and, in most cases, eventually die. It is never wise to plant any of the mint varieties in the same container as other herbs. In most cases the mint will overgrow the entire pot. Sink a pot of mint into a bed or border if possible where it will be unable to spread due to the confines of the pot. When harvesting, take the big leaves and leave the small ones. Some herbs, like coriander (cilantro), will hold up well through two or three cuttings and then they "bolt," or go to seed. Once this happens the leaves are not as flavourful. It's best to pull the plant up if this happens and start a new one every few weeks.

Fruits and berries

Many ordinary fruit trees and bushes can be grown in pots (for example, pears, apples, and blueberries). However, one of the most delightful of harvests can be from mini fruit trees. There are special varieties of fruits like apples, pears, peaches, cherries and nectarines available in this form. Not all garden centres or nurseries carry this form of tree so you may need to buy them from a mail order supply.

Containers

Clay pots are heavy and stable, but are prone to drying out, plastic is durable, light and easier to manage. For most fruit, choose pots 30-38cm/12-15in in diameter. Cherries may need 40-45cm/16-18in pots.

Planting & watering

When planting, place plenty of crocks over the base to ensure good drainage. Use a good-quality compost (John Innes No 3 is ideal), or multi-purpose compost mixed with one-third grit or perlite ensuring good soil drainage. Incorporate controlled-release fertilizer pellets in this mix, or feed fortnightly with a high-potassium liquid tomato feed.

Water generously but allow the compost's surface to dry out before the next watering, without it becoming bone dry.

To avoid pot-bound plants, re-pot every year or alternate years after leaf fall. Once in its final pot, a plant can be root-pruned every other year with 30 percent of the compost refreshed. In intervening years, replace the top layer of compost with a fresh layer.

Positioning

Position fruit plants in full sun. Leave hardy fruit outdoors over winter. Peaches and apricots should be covered with a lean-to shelter or similar, from autumn to late winter, to protect them from rain-splash and potential peach leaf curl.

Grapes

Perhaps you hadn't thought about growing grapes, but in limited space, grapes can be grown as standards, rather than climbers. Standards in a container can be moved into a heated greenhouse or conservatory if possible, when fruiting, to aid ripening.

For cultivating outdoors, it is generally best to purchase varieties that in most years perform well, even without glass protection. Grapes are still considered a luxury, which makes growing them in your own garden really worthwhile. Space can usually be found for a vine in a small garden. Try to find a south-facing spot for the vine – if possible against a sunny wall.

Ornamental varieties of grapes

Vines with decorative leaves that become richly coloured in autumn may be chosen for containers. The foliage forms splendid contrasts of purples and reds on vines covering fences and walls. The foliage of Vitis vinifera 'Purpurea' turn from red to purple, while the leaves of V. Brandt are a more orange-pink, and the grapes purple and sweet.

It is quite possible to grow a vine in a pot and produce grapes regularly every year. Vines in containers may be trained in several ways - the same as in the ground - but they do look especially attractive when raised as standards.

To maintain a healthy plant, top-dress every spring – i.e. remove around 1-2ins/3.5cm of compost from the top and replace it with fresh garden compost. Choose soil-based compost (John Innes Compost No.3) and add extra grit to help with easy drainage. Regular watering and feeding during the growing season will be required.

Strawberries

Strawberries are one of the easiest fruits to grow in containers, and are a particular favourite with children. They key, as with most containers, is the quality of the soil and regular watering and drainage. Even novice gardeners can expect great triumph in the container growing of strawberries.

Containers

Many people buy a terracotta pots designed for growing strawberries, with special pockets on the sides for multiple strawberry plants. But these can be as expensive as they are unnecessary - a friend of mine has recently grown strawberries in an old length of plastic guttering!

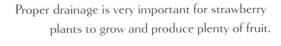

Proper drainage is very important for strawberry plants to grow and produce plenty of fruit.

You can either plant them in hanging containers or raise the containers to allow drainage. Any type of planter pots that have drainage holes in the bottom and saucers to keep the soil from washing away will work.

Planting & watering

Strawberries like soil that is loamy, with lots organic material they can consume. Your plants will need plenty of room to ensure the roots are covered. Unless you have very large containers, put only one plant in each container. Strawberry plants should be about two feet apart from each other so that they get plenty of sunlight.

Don't over water your container strawberries - they should be watered enough to keep the soil damp but not so much that you have any standing water. It is important to be sure your containers are able to drain easily without the soil being washed away.

Fertilizing container grown strawberries throughout the summer months. Fertilize your plants every other week with a high phosphorus liquid fertilizer to encourage them to flower.

Maintenance

The key to healthy tasty vegetables lies in the soil and the best way to ensure healthy, bountiful yields is to look after your soil. The tools that you will need for soil cultivation are:

Spade

This can be a back-breaking task so make it easier for yourself by ensuring that the blade is kept clean and sharp. This way it will slide through the soil and reduce the amount of effort needed. The best spades are stainless steel as the soil does not stick to the surface.

Fork

For turning the soil and ridding the soil of weeds.

Rake

This will break down the soil and allow for easy sowing of seeds and planting. Raking will also remove large stones and weed debris, although be careful you do not push the weeds back into the surface of the soil.

Trowel

You need a trowel for digging holes for individual plantings and also for removing the roots of weeds.

Compost

This will add organic matter to your soil and supply the plot with the essential nutrients needed for growing. Compost also improves soil texture and encourages the growth of micro-organisms which benefit the soil. Adding compost to your soil will also help moisture balance.

Green manure

A green manure is a type of cover crop grown primarily to add nutrients and organic matter to the soil. Typically, a green manure crop is grown for a specific period, and then ploughed under and incorporated into the soil. Green manures are ideal whenever a patch of land is going to be free of crops for six weeks or more and they are ideal when sown in the autumn to overwinter, when vegetable plots are generally empty.

Green manures usually perform multiple functions that include soil improvement and soil protection. Leguminous green manures such as clover contain nitrogen-fixing symbiotic bacteria in root nodules that fix atmospheric nitrogen in a form that plants can use, giving a boost to the vegetables that follow.

Green manures increase organic matter in the soil, thereby improving water retention, aeration, and other soil characteristics.

The root systems of some varieties of green manure grow deep in the soil and bring up nutrient resources unavailable to shallow-rooted crops. Historically, the practice of green manuring can be traced back to the fallow cycle of crop rotation, which was used to allow soils to recover.

Popular plants for green manure are mustard, clove, rye and buckwheat. Clover is a green manure that can be left to grow for a year - when it flowers it attracts bees and other pollinating insects.

Compost

For the best results, use a mixture of types of ingredient, but there is no specific recipe for creating great compost - the right balance is something you can only learn by experience, but try not to use too much of any single "ingredient".

In general, all organic matter - that is material that was once alive - can be used in creating a compost, but some are better than others.

It is possible to buy compost bins, many of which are compact and ideal for a smaller vegetable patch. A compost bin will also ensure that compost is not spread around your garden by foraging pests or even pets!

Here are a few tips to creating your first compost heap.

Activators:-

Comfrey leaves, young weeds (before they go to seed), grass cuttings.

Other compostable items include: Wood ash, cardboard egg boxes, fruit and vegetable scraps (though adding cooked food and meat products should be avoided as this can attract rats); tea bags, coffee grounds, old flowers and bedding plants, young hedge clippings and soft prunings.

Items that are "slow cookers" i.e slow to rot are:-

Autumn leaves, tough hedge clippings, woody prunings, sawdust and wood shavings.

Making your own compost is relatively simple, and whilst turning is not essential, it speeds up the process by adding air to the mix and aiding heat distribution.

Create your compost heap by adding around 30-45cm (12-18in) of your chosen waste ingredients and then cover with about 7cm (3in) of garden soil. Continue the layers at the same ratio as you build up the heap.

Turn the heap, side to middle and top to bottom, when it is about half full and then again when it is full. Cover with an old piece of carpet or strong plastic and wait for the heap to rot down, which should take a few months.

Ensure that the compost does not become too dry and that it has a regular supply of air or else nasty smells will begin to emit from your heap and the texture of the compost will be slimy.

Weeding

The key thing to remember is
that some weeds can be
tolerated in your plot
without causing major
damage to your crops, but
weeds will compete with your
crops for water, nutrients, light
and space which are all essential for
healthy plants.

Weeds can also provide information about your soil.
Poppies and pansies like chalk soil; docks like fertile soil whereas clovers are a sign
of poor fertility. Sorrel and plaintains suggest high levels of acidity in your soil.

All but the very tenacious of weeds can be smothered and killed off with a sheet of
mulch. Cut the weeds down and cover with cardboard or lots of newspaper. On top
of this spread about a 10cm (4in) layer of manure or compost. Leave in place for at
least a month and then make planting holes and fill with old compost to rejuvenate
the soil.

You can also purchase black mulching film from most garden centres and nurseries
and this will last several seasons and is many gardeners not so secret weapon
against the onset of persistant weeds.

Whilst it is probably your desire to run an organic garden, you may feel the need to
use a weedkiller such as glyphosate but be cautious of the potential harm that this
can cause to adjacent plots and discuss with your neighbouring gardeners before
application.

Crop rotation will also help reduce the growth of weeds as certain crops, for
instance potatoes, are sturdy and will efficiently crowd out weeds whilst they grow.
Rotating crops also means that it is less likely that weeds will build up in a particular
area of your plot.

Regular hoeing will also help keep the weeds on your plot at bay. Use a Dutch or stirrup hoe and keep the blade sharp. The technique to follow is to push the blade along the soil surface which will sever the weed stems from their roots. Whenever possible, hoe on a sunny day when the surface of the soil is dry so the cut weeds will quickly die.

If the soil is moist, one of the more satisfying jobs on an allotment is to pull the weeds from the soil using your hands, ensuring that you get the root out. Be aware that soil disturbance can cause more weeds, so try to pull the weeds from the soil as cleanly as possible and remember to remove the weeds from the site. If left lying on the surface of the soil, particularly in moist conditions, it is likely the weeds will root and grow again.

Pests & diseases

Vegetables can seem particularly prone to garden pests and one of the best ways to protect the health of your plants is to use preventative measures.

Ensure that your plants are strong and healthy, as whilst they will be no less prone to insect infestation, they will be better equipped to fight this than weaker plants. The main pests in the vegetable garden are of course insects, though birds, small mammals and molluscs can also cause problems.

Plant debris can provide a breeding ground for pests, so ensure that you clear away all organic litter from your beds too. Inspect your plants regularly so that you can catch problem pests at an early stage - often if you find a plant being attacked, you can "nip this in the bud" so to speak by removing the damaged leaf or growing tip.

Tell tale signs of pest attack are plants not performing as well as others. Wilting leaves and a slimy trail left by snails and slugs are signs of root damage.

You can protect your root vegetables by creating a physical barrier by using polythene or fine netting erected about 1m (3ft) high around your plants.

This will deter snails and slugs, plus carrot and onion flies which travel close to the ground guided by smell.

Remember that if you are trying to protect your plot from burrowing animals, such as rabbits, you will need to place any fencing at least 30cm (12in) underground.

You can protect individual plants by cutting the bases from large plastic drinking bottles and placing the top over the plant, with the cap removed.

Cloches are also a very effective, though more costly, protective barrier, particularly when plants are young.

Another tip is that certain insects (aphids) and birds can be dazzled by strips of aluminium foil. In the case of aphids, run strips of foil alongside your plants to deter them by disorientation.

Moving strips of foil or even old cd's tied to a string help deter birds.

If you find that despite preventative measures your plants still succumb to pests, there are many ways that you can tackle this problem. Depending upon the scale of the problem and the pest, it is often possible to remove them easily enough by picking them off by hand - but don't throw back on to the plot if you can help it, place them in a container and remove from the site.

It is also possible to dislodge insects by spraying with water, but be careful that the jet is not too strong or this may damage the plant. Given that a lot of pests are attracted by the smell of the vegetables, many repellents contain extracts of citrus of garlic to confuse the pests.

In the case of slugs and snails, sink a deep sided dish of beer or special slug attractant into the ground at soil level which will lure the pests in and drown them.

Most commercial pesticides are non-organic and so may not be appealing in your quest for healthy home-grown vegetables, but you need to take into account that all of these will have had to pass stringent tests to ensure they cause no harm to the user. However, they will be harmful to all insects - not just pests, as they do not discriminate between good and bad insects.

You can also look for environment-friendly products which have a low toxicity and break down quickly after use.

Another method is to grow plants that attract "good" insects that will feed upon the pests. Pest controlling insects include hoverflies, lacewings and ladybirds and plants which attract these are golden marguerite (daisy), marigolds, coriander, buckwheat, fennel and lemon balm.

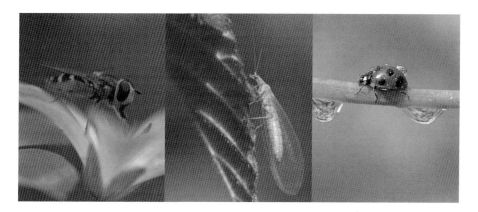

Hoverfly   Lacewing   Ladybird

A number of pests, such as the carrot fly and onion fly, search for plants using their evolved sense of smell. Excessive handling of plants can release scents into the air, thereby attracting these insects.

Wherever possible avoid excessive handling or brusing of the folliage on carrots and onions and weed or thin plants later in the day which will give the flying pests less chance to track them down. You can also grow onions and carrots along side strong-smelling plants such as garlic, to send confusing signals.

Know your pests....

There is an argument that no matter how good your preventative measures are, it will be impossibe to keep your fruit and vegetables free of pests, so once they do appear it is important that you take swift action to limit their infestation.

Soil pests	Cutworm, millipede, wireworm.
Symptoms	Feeding on the root or stem of plants causing leaves to wilt and turn yellow.
Cure or control	Dig soil in autumn and winter to expose to elements and birds.
Beetles	Asparagus beetle, flea beetle, pea weevils, bean weevils.
Symptoms	Beetles feed on the leaves and stems, biting holes in plants.
Cure or control	Handpick beetles where seen and treat with chemical controls such as Bifenthrin.
Flies	Cabbage root fly, carrot fly, onion fly, celery leaf miner.
Symptoms	Cabbage root fly early stage symptoms are often wilting of low leaves in warm weather. Larvae feed on roots. Carrot flies feed on roots, leaves of affected plants will take on a red tinge. Celery leaf miner attacks leaves causing white patches. Onion flies attack the bulb and stems causing rot.

Cure or control

Dig soil in autumn and winter to expose to elements and birds. Clear away all plant debris which can provide nesting areas for adults.

Carrot flies find carrots by smell so avoid handling the foliage as when bruised it emits a stronger smell.

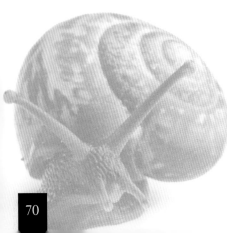

Caterpillars

Cabbage, caterpillar, pea moth, tomato moth.

Symptoms

Reduce cabbage family plants to lattice work in days. Pea moths feed unseen in the pods of developing peas. Tomato moths eat holes in both leaves and fruit of plant.

Cure or control

Inspect underside of leaves for egg clusters and remove affected leaves. Pick off caterpillars. Sow peas early or late to avoid growth during peak caterpillar season.

Mammals & birds

Deer, rabbits, mice, voles, badgers, moles, cats.

Symptoms

Mammals will generally eat plants and seeds. Pigeons attack cabbage family plants.

Cure or control

Keep garden clear of debris; erect fencing, netting and scaring devices.

Aphids

Black bean aphid, cabbage aphid, mealy cabbage aphid, potato aphid.

Symptoms

Sapsuckers which weaken plants and spoil the taste. Reproduce rapidly and exude sticky dew.

Cure or control

Keep garden clear of debris; pick off all infected leaves and shoots; spray with water jets to remove.

Slugs and Snails

Field slug, garden slug, keeled slug, garden snail.

Symptoms

Generally night feeders, they eat through leaves and stems and can eat seedlings whole.

Cure or control

Use a slug and snail trap; wearing gloves to protect your hands from slime, pick off plants. Surround individual plants with sharp sand or crushed eggshell.

Know your diseases....

Having spent time creating your vegetable patch or allotment, it is important to ensure that your vegetables are kept healthy, so beware of these common diseases which could affect your crops. Bolting, when vegetables run to seed triggered normally by a cold snapt, can be one of the most common problems and is best tackled by looking for bolt resistant cultivars - an example being "Boltardy" beetroot.

Blight	Affects potatoes and tomatoes.
Symptoms	Occurring in warm wet weather, first signs are dark blotches on leaves followed by wilting and yellowing foliage and stem, followed by the collapse of the plant. In tomatoes, leaves collapse and the fruit develops brown rotting patches.
Cure or control	During early stages on potato foliage, remove and burn the topgrowth. Destroy infected or suspect crops by burning or burying well away from your plot.
Blossom-end rot	Affects tomatoes and peppers.
Symptoms	A dry sunken decay on the blossom end (opposite stem end) caused by a shortage of calcium.
Cure or control	Keep the soil moist but avoid large fluctuations in soil moisture by using mulches.
Botrytis (grey mould)	Many crops are affected, but lettuce and tomatoes are particularly susceptible.
Symptoms	Fungus starts on dead tissue but spreads through out the plant producing fluffy grey mould.
Cure or control	Clear dead and dying plant debris promptly, and cut out and destroy affected parts of the plant.

Canker

Affects carrots.

Symptoms   Shoulders of the roots become dark brown and shrivelled.

Cure or control Worse during damp seasons and acid soil. Follow a crop rotation plan and add lime to the soil where necessary.

Club root

Affects the cabbage family plants.

Symptoms   Roots swell and become distorted. Plants are stunted and wilt in warm weather. Favouring moist, warm acid soils, this disease creates spores as the roots rot which can lay dormant for many years.

Cure or control Crop rotation does not help, but sowing during the cooler season reduces the risk of attack. Raise plants in pots using sterile compost then plant out with roots in a good ball of compost.

Damping off

Affects all seedlings.

Symptoms   Lesions appear on stems and seedlings collapse.

Cure or control Use sterile compost, keep trays ventilated and minimise overcrowding.

Leaf & pod spots

Affects beans, cabbage family plants and cucumbers.

Symptoms   Spots on foliage and stems.

Cure or control Keep your plot free of debris and destroy affected leaves.

Mildew

Affects cabbage family plants, peas, onions, lettuce and spinach.

Symptoms

Powdery and downy mildew produces a white or grey mould, often in round patches. Not fluffy like botrytis.

Cure or control

Do not over water or over crowd plants.

Scab

Affects potatoes.

Symptoms

Tubers have brown, round cork areas on surface.

Cure or control

Do not lime soil before growing potatoes. Keep plants moist during prolonged dry spells.

Virus

Affects cabbage family plants, lettuce, potatoes and tomatoes.

Symptoms

Malformed leaves with crinkled or rolled edges.
Mottling patterns on leaves.

Cure or control

Aphids are the main carriers of viruses so control aphids and ensure that equipment is kept clean. Remove and burn affected plants.

Wilt

Affects tomatoes and cabbage family plants.

Symptoms

The most common type is Fusarium where young plants become pale and stunted. Low leaves wilt and as the symptoms move upwards, plants are killed off. Fusarium wilt can often infect only one side of the plant. Verticillium wilt causes similar symptoms but without the one-sided effect.

Cure or control

Wilt diseases are worse in hot weather, and can stay in the soil. Clear away plant debris and follow crop rotation and try growing resistant varieties.

Recipes

Having grown and harvested your own delicious home produce, here are a selection
of recipes to bring out their best flavours.

Spicy Beetroot & Coconut Soup (Serves 6)

Ingredients

500g/1lb 2oz raw beetroot
2 tbsps vegetable oil
2 shallots, finely chopped
1 tsp cumin seeds
570ml/1 pint vegetable stock
1 tin x 400ml coconut milk
pinch sea salt

Ingredients for paste

2 lemon grass stalks
2 cloves garlic, peeled
3 red chillies
5cm fresh ginger root, peeled
4 kaffir lime leaves
1 lime, juiced

Ingredients for serving

1 tbsp fresh mint
1 tbsp fresh coriander leaves
small cucumber, deseeded and chopped

Method

1. Preheat the oven to 200C/400F/Gas 6. Sprinkle the beets with 1 tbsp of
vegetable oil and season with sea salt. Wrap them in kitchen foil, place in a roasting
tin and cook for 35 minutes until tender. Once cooled, peel and chop.

2. For the paste, peel the tough outer coating from the lemon grass stalks, then
finely chop the white bulbous part of each stalk, discarding the rest.

3. Put the lemon grass, garlic, chillies, ginger, lime leaves and lime juice in a blender
and blend until smooth.

Spicy Beetroot & Coconut Soup/cont.

4. Heat the remaining vegetable oil in a saucepan, add the shallots and cumin seeds and fry gently for 2-3 minutes.

5. Add half the paste and fry for 5 minutes, stirring to ensure good coverage. Add the roast beetroot and fry for a further 2 minutes. Pour in the vegetable stock and bring to the boil before simmering for about 7-8 minutes.

6. Just before serving, put the soup, coconut milk and remaining paste mix into a blender and blend until smooth. Pour into 6 dishes, sprinkle the top with finely chopped cucumber - tear the mint and coriander leaves into small pieces and place on top. Serve with warm bread.

Broccoli & Bacon Frittata (Serves 2)

Ingredients

1/2 medium sized broccoli, cut into florets
200g/7 oz linguine, cooked al dente
4 rashers bacon, chopped
1/2 onion, chopped
1 tbsps olive oil
3 free-range eggs, lightly beaten
salt and freshly ground black pepper

Method

1. Cook the linguine following the packet instructions and set aside. Heat the oil in a small frying pan and fry the bacon until crisp. Add the onion and fry until softened.

2. Add the broccoli and fry for 3-4 minutes, stirring frequently, until softened. Add the linguine to the pan. Season the eggs with salt and freshly ground black pepper and pour into the pan.

3. Cook over a medium heat until the base is set and golden-brown, then carefully cover the frying pan with a plate and turn the frittata out onto the plate. Slide the frittata back into the pan and cook until browned on the other side. To serve, cut the frittata into wedges and place onto serving plates.

Sour Cream & Chive Dip (Serves 4)
Ingredients

3 tbsps fresh chives, chopped

3 tbsps sour cream

1 tsp lemon juice

pinch of sea salt

Method

1. Mix all of the ingredients together in a bowl and chill. Serve with raw vegetables (washed and cut straight from the garden!)

Alioli (Serves 4)
Ingredients

5 garlic cloves, crushed

250-300ml/1/2 pint olive oil

1 egg yolk

1 egg

pinch of salt, generous

Method

1. Place the eggs, garlic and salt in a food processor and process them for a few seconds until well combined.

2. Slowly pour in the olive oil with the motor running until the alioli has thickened to a mayonnaise consistency. Serve the alioli as soon as it is prepared with warm crusty bread.

Kale with Horseradish (Serves 8)
Ingredients

400g/14oz curly kale, washed and chopped

25g/1oz butter

3-4 tbsps hot horseradish

Method

1. Set a wok over a high heat – you may need to use two, depending on their size. Add the wet curly kale and cover with a tight-fitting lid. Cook for 5 minutes, stirring occasionally, until soft and tender.

Kale with Horseradish/cont.

2. Add the butter and horseradish to the pan and toss through the curly kale. Season to taste and serve immediately.

Kohlrabi Stir-fry (Serves 4)

Ingredients

1 kohlrabi, peeled and cut into thin sticks

1 large carrot, peeled and cut into thin sticks

2 tbsps sesame oil

2cm piece fresh root ginger, grated

1 clove garlic, crushed

250g/9oz pack thread egg noodles

1 bunch salad onions, diagonally sliced

125g/4 1/2oz sugar snap peas, topped and tailed

3-4 tbsps hoi sin sauce

2 tbsps soy sauce

2 tbsps water

1 tsp peanut butter

2 tbsps sesame seeds

Method

1. Heat the sesame oil in a large wok then add the ginger, garlic, kohlrabi and carrot then stir-fry for 3-4 minutes.

2. Soak the noodles in boiling water to reconstitute, following instructions on the packet. Add the salad onions and sugar snap peas to the wok. Stir-fry for a further 1-2 minutes. Stir in the hoi sin sauce, soy sauce, water, peanut butter and half the sesame seeds.

3. Stir in the reconsitituted, drained noodles and serve immediately sprinkled with the remaining sesame seeds.

Pea & Mint Soup (Serves 4)
Ingredients
900g/2 lb peas in the pod, shelled to about 250g/9oz peas
50g/2oz fresh mint, chopped
1 bunch spring onions, trimmed and roughly chopped
1 potato, peeled and diced
1 garlic clove, crushed
850ml/1 1/4 pint vegetable or chicken stock
large pinch sugar
1 tbsp fresh lemon juice
150ml/1/4 pint soured cream

Method
1. In a large pan, place the stock, potato, garlic and spring onions then bring to the boil. Allow to simmer for 15 minutes or until the potato is very soft.

2. Add the peas to the soup base and simmer for no longer than 5 minutes to retain the sweet, fresh flavour. Next add the chopped mint, sugar and lemon juice and stir well.

3. Remove from the heat and allow to cool for about 5 minutes before placing in a blender and blending until smooth. Stir in half of soured cream, taste and season with salt and pepper.

4. Return to the pan, and return to the heat to warm through gently (be careful here if your soup is too hot the sour cream will curdle). Once warmed, serve the soup with warm crusty wholemeal bread.

Roasted Sesame Radishes (Serves 4)

Ingredients

24 radishes, leaves, stems, and roots trimmed

1 tsp of sesame oil

2 tbsps soy sauce

6 medium-sized spring onions, thinly sliced

1 tbsp sesame seeds, toasted

handful of chopped coriander

rocket leaves for garnish, optional

Method

1. Preheat the oven to 200C/400F/Gas 6. Slice the radishes in half lengthways. Toss the halved radishes with the peanut oil on a baking sheet.

2. Roast for 25 minutes, turning once or twice, until the radishes are tender and beginning to brown. Drizzle the soy sauce over the roasted radishes and toss with the spring onion.

3. Roast for a further 5 minutes. Transfer to a serving bowl. Sprinkle with the sesame seeds and coriander, garnish with the rocket and serve.

Traditional Rhubarb Crumble (Serves 4)

Ingredients

450g/1 lb rhubarb

55ml/2 fl oz water

110g/4oz caster sugar

200g/7oz plain flour

110g/4oz cold butter, cubed

125g/4 1/2oz demerara sugar

Method

1. Preheat the oven to 180C/350F/Gas mark 4. Trim the rhubarb into pieces (3cm in length) and place in a ovenproof dish. Sprinkle over the water and caster sugar.

2. Sift the flour into a bowl, add the cold, cubed butter and rub in with your fingertips until the mixture resembles breadcrumbs. Stir in the sugar.

3. Spread the crumble topping over the rhubarb then bake for 35-40 minutes or until the top is golden brown and the rhubarb bubbling through at the edges. Serve with cream, custard or ice cream.

Potato & Spinach Skins with Poached Eggs (Serves 4)

Ingredients

4 large baking potatoes
225g/8oz spinach
8 rashers of streaky bacon
knob of butter
1 shallot, finely diced
3 tbsps tarragon white wine vinegar
3 tbsp white wine
150ml/1/4 pint double cream
175g/6oz unsalted butter
25g/1oz chives
150ml/1/4 pint crème fraîche
salt and ground black pepper

Ingredients for poached eggs

4 large eggs
4 tbsp white wine vinegar, for poaching eggs

Method

1. Scrub the potatoes, pierce them with a fork and bake at 200C/400F/Gas 6 for 1 hour or until they are soft inside and crispy outside. Cut a slice off the top of each potato and scoop out the insides. Rub the insides with a little butter, place the skins on a baking tray and return them to the oven for 10 minutes. Grill bacon until crisp.

2. Next, place the shallot, vinegar and wine in a small saucepan and reduce by two thirds. Add the double cream and cook for 3 minutes before straining through a fine sieve. Cut the butter into small cubes and add gradually, off the heat, using a balloon whisk. The sauce should be thick and glossy. Season to taste and add the chopped chives just before serving.

3. Sauté the spinach and drain well. Combine with the crème fraîche and season to taste. Place a little in the bottom of each potato skin.

Potato & Spinach Skins with Poached Eggs/cont.

4. Poach the eggs in a shallow pan of simmering water with a little vinegar. Remove and drain well on kitchen paper. Place an egg on top of the spinach mixture in each potato skin, spoon some sauce over the egg and top with a cross of crispy bacon. The plate can be garnished with a few chives.

Pickled Onions (Makes 1 large jar)

Ingredients

1kg/2 1/4lb small onions or shallots
30g/1oz salt
1 tsp dried chilli flakes
1 ltr/1 3/4 pint malt vinegar
180g/6oz granulated sugar

Method

1. Peel the onions then place in a large bowl with the salt and mix together. Cover and leave overnight. Rinse well in cold water and allow to dry thoroughly.

2. Place the onions into a large sterilised jar. In a saucepan, slowly bring to the boil the vinegar, chilli flakes and sugar until the sugar has disolved.

3. Pour the vinegar mix over the onions and seal the jars then store in a cool, dark cupboard for at least two weeks before eating.

Roasted Turnip Soup with Honey Cream (Serves 4)

Ingredients

900g/2 lbs turnips, peeled and cut into 1-inch chunks

1 large onion, diced

6 garlic cloves, peeled

1 leek, washed well and chopped

1 tsp dried thyme

4 tbsps olive oil

275ml/1/2 pint vegetable or chicken stock

2 cups milk

salt and black pepper for seasoning

Ingredients for honey cream

150ml/1/4 pint sour cream

2 tsps double cream

1 tbsp honey

Method

1. Preheat your oven to 200C/400F/Gas 6. Bring a large pot of lightly salted water to boil. Blanch the turnips for 3 minute then drain and rinse with cold water. Lightly towel dry the turnips.

2. Toss the turnips, onions, leeks, garlic and thyme in oil in a large bowl. Spread on a baking tray in a single layer then roast for approximately 1 hour, stirring and turning every 15 minute or so until browned evenly.

3. Place the roasted vegetables in a large saucepan. Add the stock and milk to the pan and season well. Bring almost to the boil and partially cover. Reduce the heat to simmer and cook for about 30 minutes or until the turnips are quite tender. Allow the soup to cool and then place in a blender and blend to desired consisteny. This is best done in batches.

4. To make the honey cream, mix all of the ingredients together well then spoon on top of the soup and serve with fresh warm bread.

Parsnip & Nut Mash (Serves 8)

Ingredients

1.5kg/3 1/2lb parsnips
700g/1lb 9oz potatoes
75g/3oz walnuts
75g/3oz butter
3 tbsps sesame oil
100ml/4fl oz vegetable oil, for frying
salt and black pepper for seasoning

Method

1. Lightly toast and roughly chop the walnuts. Cut 3 of the parsnips in half lengthways, then slice each half into 3 wedges. Cut the potatoes and remaining parsnips into chunky pieces and place in a large saucepan of cold water with the parsnip wedges on top.

2. Bring to the boil, reduce the heat and simmer gently for 5-6 minutes or until the parsnip wedges have softened. Remove the wedges with a slotted spoon and cook the remaining vegetables for 10-15 minutes. Drain and return to the pan.

3. Mash the vegetables in the pan until smooth. Add the butter and sesame oil, and stir until thoroughly combined. Season to taste.

4. Heat the vegetable oil in a large frying pan and gently fry the parsnip wedges until golden, turning them frequently to avoid burning. Drain on kitchen paper. Put the mash onto a serving plate and scatter with the nuts.

Planting diary

Keeping a record of when you plant, what you plant, where you plant, the estimated yield and harvest time will enable you to get the most out of your vegetable patch or allotment and to plan your budgeting and time in the garden effectively.

It is essential that you record the position in the plot or patch if you are planning on incorporating a crop rotation system to best benefit your soil.

Crop _____ Date _____

Variety _____

Position in plot/patch _____

Estimated yield _____

Estimated time of harvest _____

Comment _____

Crop _____ Date _____

Variety _____

Position in plot/patch _____

Estimated yield _____

Estimated time of harvest _____

Comment _____

Crop _____ Date _____

Variety _____

Position in plot/patch _____

Estimated yield _____

Estimated time of harvest _____

Comment _____

_____

Crop _____ Date _____

Variety _____

Position in plot/patch _____

Estimated yield _____

Estimated time of harvest _____

Comment _____

_____

Crop _____ Date _____

Variety _____

Position in plot/patch _____

Estimated yield _____

Estimated time of harvest _____

Comment _____

_____

Crop _____   Date _____

Variety _____

Position in plot/patch _____

Estimated yield _____

Estimated time of harvest _____

Comment _____

_____

Crop _____   Date _____

Variety _____

Position in plot/patch _____

Estimated yield _____

Estimated time of harvest _____

Comment _____

_____

Crop _____   Date _____

Variety _____

Position in plot/patch _____

Estimated yield _____

Estimated time of harvest _____

Comment _____

_____

Crop _____ Date _____

Variety _____

Position in plot/patch _____

Estimated yield _____

Estimated time of harvest _____

Comment _____

_____

Crop _____ Date _____

Variety _____

Position in plot/patch _____

Estimated yield _____

Estimated time of harvest _____

Comment _____

_____

Crop _____ Date _____

Variety _____

Position in plot/patch _____

Estimated yield _____

Estimated time of harvest _____

Comment _____

_____

Crop _____ Date _____

Variety _____

Position in plot/patch _____

Estimated yield _____

Estimated time of harvest _____

Comment _____

_____

Crop _____ Date _____

Variety _____

Position in plot/patch _____

Estimated yield _____

Estimated time of harvest _____

Comment _____

_____

Crop _____ Date _____

Variety _____

Position in plot/patch _____

Estimated yield _____

Estimated time of harvest _____

Comment _____

_____

Crop _____ Date _____

Variety _____

Position in plot/patch _____

Estimated yield _____

Estimated time of harvest _____

Comment _____

_____

Crop _____ Date _____

Variety _____

Position in plot/patch _____

Estimated yield _____

Estimated time of harvest _____

Comment _____

_____

Crop _____ Date _____

Variety _____

Position in plot/patch _____

Estimated yield _____

Estimated time of harvest _____

Comment _____

_____

Crop _____ Date _____

Variety _____

Position in plot/patch _____

Estimated yield _____

Estimated time of harvest _____

Comment _____

_____

Crop _____ Date _____

Variety _____

Position in plot/patch _____

Estimated yield _____

Estimated time of harvest _____

Comment _____

_____

Crop _____ Date _____

Variety _____

Position in plot/patch _____

Estimated yield _____

Estimated time of harvest _____

Comment _____

Crop   Date

Variety

Position in plot/patch

Estimated yield

Estimated time of harvest

Comment

Crop   Date

Variety

Position in plot/patch

Estimated yield

Estimated time of harvest

Comment

Crop   Date

Variety

Position in plot/patch

Estimated yield

Estimated time of harvest

Comment

INDEX

The recipes contained in this book are passed on in good faith but the publisher cannot be held responsible for any adverse results. Please be aware that certain recipes may contain nuts. The recipes use both metric and imperial measurements, and the reader should not mix metric and imperial measurements. Spoon measurements are level, teaspoons are assumed to be 5ml, tablespoons 15ml. For other measurements, see chart below. Times given are for guidance only, as preparation techniques may vary and can lead to different cooking times.

Grams to ounces

10g	0.25oz	225g	8oz
15g	0.38oz	250g	9oz
25g	1oz	275g	10oz
50g	2oz	300g	11oz
75g	3oz	350g	12oz
110g	4oz	375g	13oz
150g	5oz	400g	14oz
175g	6oz	425g	15oz
200g	7oz	450g	16oz

Spoons to millilitres

1/2 teaspoon	2.5 ml	1 Tablespoon	15 ml
1 teaspoon	5 ml	2 Tablespoons	30 ml
1-1 1/2 teaspoons	7.5 ml	3 Tablespoons	45 ml
2 teaspoons	10 ml	4 Tablespoons	60 ml

Metric to cups

Description		
Flour etc	115g	1 cup
Clear honey etc	350g	1 cup
Liquids etc	225ml	1 cup

Liquid measures

5fl oz	1/4 pint	150 ml
7.5fl oz		215 ml
10fl oz	1/2 pint	275 ml
15fl oz		425 ml
20fl oz	1 pint	570 ml
35fl oz		1 litre

Oven Temperatures

Gas mark	°F	°C
1	275°F	140°C
2	300°F	150°C
3	325°F	170°C
4	350°F	180°C
5	375°F	190°C
6	400°F	200°C
7	425°F	220°C
8	450°F	230°C
9	475°F	240°C

The photographs in this book are for illustrative purposes only and do not represent the finished recipe. Photographs © Getty Images, Jupiter Images, Image Source and Shutterstock. All rights reserved. No part of this publication may be reproduced, stored in a retrieval system or transmitted by any means (electronic, mechanical, photocopying or otherwise) without the prior permission of the publisher.